"In **BURNING DAYLIGHT**, Jamie Holden urges men to rise to the challenge of living out the Great Commission, reminding us that there is a real heaven and a real hell, and that we must commit ourselves to the task of communicating biblically-based convictions over these two eternal destinations.

Jamie's book is the cry of the evangelist to engage in the call to evangelism. It is refreshing to read a book dedicated to inspiring believers in general, and believing men in particular, to participate in God's mission...the mission of presenting the good news to those who are lost in a world engulfed in darkness and hopelessness.

Jamie's encouragement to rise to the missional challenge (engage) and shine without obstruction (live out our witness in purity and spiritual vibrancy) is a necessary message for every man of faith to embrace. Let's ALL *"Rise and Shine!"*

-**Dr. Don Immel,** *PennDel Ministry Network Superintendent*

"As I read **BURNING DAYLIGHT** I thought, *"With Rocky, Batman and Iron Man, this is definitely a men's book."* Like the characters he writes about, I believe that Jamie is a modern-day superhero! Despite a disability and physical pain that would make most people stay in bed, Jamie pushes through with courage to confront complacency and help men RISE and SHINE.

I highly recommend **BURNING DAYLIGHT** as a tool for your men's ministry. The group study questions and personal workbook will challenge your men to RISE in godliness and SHINE through the darkness!"

-**Tom Rees,** *PennDel Ministry Network Men's Director*

"**BURNING DAYLIGHT** explores an in-depth Biblical view of what it means to live for Jesus. Jamie lays out a Biblical systematic solution to having Christ-centered success in ones personal ministry and life. This book will challenge Christians to evaluate their walk with the Lord as the steps to godly living are unraveled in every chapter."

–**Phil Menditto,** *Founder and Senior Pastor, Philadelphia Christian Center*

"Jamie doesn't pull any punches as he calls and challenges men across America to rise up and step into their call. If you're looking to be coddled, this book isn't for you. However, if you're done with complacency, then I highly recommend this work to you."

-**Jason Tourville,** *PennDel Ministry Network Director of Minister Care and Church Recalibration*

"For those looking for encouragement as well as informative instruction for their daily lives, **BURNING DAYLIGHT** by Jamie Holden, is for you. Jamie has a well written book, that will inspire, encourage and meet all of us on our journey from here to glory. Jamie's book hits us right where we are."

-**Pastor Walter Smith,** *abundantLIFEchurch, South Central West Sectional Presbyter for the Penn-Del District Council of the A/G*

BURNING DAYLIGHT

THE GODLY MAN'S CALL TO RISE AND SHINE.

James J. Holden

Published by 4One Ministries, Inc. Visit www.mantourministries.com for more information on bulk discounts and special promotions, or e-mail your questions to info@4oneministries.org.

Design: James J. Holden
The author wishes to recognize Adessa Holden for her contribution to the text as an integral part of 4One Ministries, Adessa has participated in numerous editorial sessions and has willing shared her words during the creation of this work to advance God's Kingdom.
Subject Headings:
1. Christian life 2. Men's Ministry 3. Spiritual Growth

ISBN 978-1-7338505-8-2
ISBN 978-1-7338505-9-9 (ebook)
Printed in the United States of America

DEDICATION

This book is dedicated to all the men who faithfully have attended the Mantour Conferences and supported Mantour Ministries. When I started this ministry so many years ago, I had many tell me that men will not take time on a Saturday morning to attend a men's conference. They said men aren't that into men's ministry, reading, or being part of a men's movement.

You have proven them wrong as each of you make it a point to go to your local Mantour, hungry for more of God. You all inspire me to press on through hard times, pain, and struggles. I write and dedicate this book to you.

TABLE OF CONTENTS

1. THE DIMMER SWITCH   9

   PART ONE: RISE

2. A WAKE UP CALL   17

3. YOU SNOOZE, THEY LOSE   25

4. STAYING UP   35

5. GETTING DRESSED PART 1   43

6. GETTING DRESSED PART 2   59

7. STANDING FIRM   69

   PART TWO: SHINING BRIGHT

8. FEELING DARKNESS   83

9. SHINING FOR LIFE   93

10. OLD TIME RELIGION   111

11. SHINE A LIGHT ON HEALING   121

12. CONCLUSION   137

    WORKBOOK   149

    FILL IN ANSWERS   183

    BIBLIOGRAPHY   185

CHAPTER ONE
THE DIMMER SWITCH

I've never been a morning person. Even as a child, my mom had to drag me out of bed. Every Christmas morning, I frustrated my older sister because she had to come into my room, wake me up, and practically carry me to the living room to open her presents.

Mornings are tough for me; I am more of a night owl. When I was a younger man, I would stay up until 1 or 2 am. When I turned forty, for some reason, my body started changing, and my bedtime turned into 10–11:30 pm! Turning forty also made it easier to wake up because my bladder wakes me up early! However, I still struggle with really early mornings (like before the sun comes up!) When I know I have to get up at 4 or 5 am, I can hardly even sleep the night before. I wake up every hour, checking the alarm, and doing the math to see how much time I have left to sleep.

Recently, I had such a night. To save money on a hotel bill, we decided to get up super early and drive the two hours to one of our

Mantour Conferences. It took me forever to fall asleep, knowing I had to get up at 4:15 am, but eventually, I was able to doze off. When I woke up, I looked at my phone, and it said 7 am. I screamed to my sister across the hall, *"Dessa, we overslept! We won't get there in time!"* I screamed so loud that I woke myself up, and it was only 3 am! Thankfully, it was just a bad dream, and we got to the Mantour on time.

As I said, I am not a morning person. I'm not one of those people who wake up looking fantastic with a perky and chipper attitude. Instead, my crazy curls are going everywhere, I have eye crusts in the corner of my eyes, and a blank look on my face. The phrase *"rise and shine"* is not something I'd frequently say.

However, lately, I have not been able to shake those three words... *"Rise and Shine"*. They've been stirring in me for weeks.

I believe God is calling His men to rise and shine. What do I mean? Check out this verse:

> *You are the light of the world. A town built on a hill cannot be hidden. Neither do people light a lamp and put it under a bowl. Instead they put it on its stand, and it gives light to everyone in the house. In the same way, let your light shine before others, that they may see your good deeds and glorify your Father in heaven.*
> *-Matthew 5:14-16 (NIV)*

It is time for God's children to rise and shine. We are called to be a light in this dark world, to stand out, and to be different. We should stand out as much as a flashlight stands out in an electrical blackout. The world needs to see something different about us.

Notice that this verse says that we shouldn't take our light that shines brightly to the world and place it under a bowl. The old school wording is *"hide it under a bushel,"* which you'll recognize if you ever sang the song *"This Little Light of Mine."* I remember being a child in Sunday School and belting out the infamous line, *"Hide it under a bushel, NO! I'm gonna let it shine"*. It was a children's church classic, but in reality, not many of us know what a bushel is, and we don't put a light under a bowl. So what exactly is this verse saying?

The modern-day equivalent of a bushel is a dimmer switch. Dimmer switches do what their name suggests, it dims the light and makes it less bright. A year or so ago, we had some lights installed in our living room, and one of the lights is directly over the chair where I sit to watch television every night. When we had the lights installed, they asked if we wanted a dimmer switch. We never had dimmers installed on any lights in our house before, but the electrician really seemed to think we needed it, so we installed it. The first night when we sat to watch tv, I was so glad we did!

The light directly over me was SO bright…I couldn't stand it. It made a glare on my glasses, it made me feel like I was sitting under a spotlight, and it was SO HOT! This light made me so uncomfortable. I was so happy I could dim it and make it shine less bright.

While having a dimmer installed on this light in our living room was great, having dimmers installed on our spiritual light is terrible. The problem is, too many believers have installed a dimmer switch on their light. They dim the light if it is too bright for some people, or if it makes others uncomfortable, or if the world finds Christianity offensive.

But the truth is, the Gospel is offensive to a sinful world. It is truth amid lies and the standard among a world filled with compromise. It always has and always will offend, but we are called to shine on anyway. We need to shine bright.

The Holy Spirit reinforced this truth to me on New Year's Eve, as I watched the annual year in review on tv. This is our New Year's Eve tradition…put on our pj's, order a pizza, watch the year in review on a couple of different channels, and watch the ball drop (if we make it that long). Yeah, I'm a real party animal. However, this year, it was less enjoyable because the show's tone was different than it had been in past years. I was stunned as they continually called evil-good and good-evil.

These programs reinforced the truth that the world sees Christians as evil, angry, hate-filled people. They despise what we believe in, and they hate our God. They don't believe He is the only way. In their opinion, any religion is good, and most religions are better than Christianity. They hate us and the truths for which we stand.

It was a confirmation of something I believe is coming for believers. I genuinely believe persecution is in the near future for Christians. If we dim our light pre-persecution, will we extinguish it when it happens? Persecution will come. But we must shine on!

It is easy to dim our light, try and be less offensive, be more politically correct, make little compromises, not offend, and not make waves. I get it; it is sometimes just more comfortable to not upset people. But God never called us to the easy, wide road. He called us to the narrow path, the hard road. He called us to shine bright.

> ***Enter through the narrow gate. For wide is the gate and broad is the road that leads to destruction, and many enter through it. But small is the gate and narrow the road that leads to life, and only a few find it.***
> ***-Matthew 7:13-14 (NIV)***

I believe that as we move through the 2020's, God is calling us to shine bright. It's time to get rid of the dimmer switch. Many will hate us for it. However, the hidden truth I have found is that, while some will hate, others yearn for truth, righteousness, and purity. They have tried it the world's ways, and it left them beaten, battered, and hurting.

They need hope. They need peace. They need absolutes. They need what we have...the truth of the Gospel. Freedom from sin. HOPE! We have to stop dimming our light. It's time we, as believers, rise and shine!

We shine bright when we become men who not only know what the Bible says, but also, become men who do what the Bible says. We shine bright when we live the way God calls us to live because God's way is so counter-culture. Still, we must shine on because God's way is the only way. While we will stand out from the world, and a lot of people won't like the stance or positions we take, and some will even hate you for them, we must shine on.

WE HAVE TO STOP DIMMING OUR LIGHT. IT'S TIME WE, AS BELIEVERS, RISE AND SHINE!

That's what this book is designed to do, to encourage you to rise and shine. We are going to look at some of the great principles of God's Word that have been pushed aside in today's day and age. Still, these principles are as true today as they were 2,000 years ago. We need to know them, embrace them, and make them a part of our lives.

As we move forward through this book, we will discuss ways we can both *"rise"* and *"shine"*. We are breaking this book into two sections. Section one will explain what it means to *"rise"* and how we do it. The second section will focus on *"shining bright."*

Each chapter will have study questions to help you apply the words in each chapter to your life. They are also great tools to make this a men's group study with your friends or your church's men's ministry. And of course, as always, we will have a workbook in the back of the book.

I am excited to see how God will raise his men to shine bright in the world. We will rise and become all God has called us to be. Are you ready for this exciting journey? Then let's move forward together as we rise and shine.

Group Study Questions:

1. Why is it important to Rise and Shine?

2. Is there any area of your life where you are using a spiritual dimmer switch?

3. What is your greatest fear of shining bright in a dark world?

4. Is this fear rational? Or would it not be as bad as you think?

5. After reading this chapter, what is one thing you will put into practice or one thing you will change in your life?

6. How can we, as a group, help you do this?

PART ONE:

RISE

CHAPTER TWO
A WAKE UP CALL

One thing people may not know about me is that I used to play the drums. I say *"used to"* because I can't do it anymore with my disability. I wasn't a great drummer, but I could keep the beat and hold my own.

When my mom and dad signed me up for drum lessons, I hated it. The instructor was trying to teach me how to read music and play drums for an orchestra or marching band. I just wanted to be a rock star! Eventually, I convinced my instructor that I wanted to learn to play drums like a rock band, this marching band stuff wasn't for me!

My parents bought me a used drum set, and I would wail on them for hours! I would take my boom-box (Google it if you are too young to know what that is) and bang on the drums to classic Christian Rock bands like *Petra, Whiteheart,* and *Stryper.*

One of my favorite songs to play along to was *"Sleeping Giant"* by Petra. It was one of the best songs on their *"Wake Up Call"* cassette. (Again, Google *"cassette"* lol.) It had such a great beat. While all the songs on this album were great to play along to, this song was my favorite!

If you have never heard this song, check it out on Youtube…it is awesome! Even more than the sound, the lyrics have a powerful message as they talk about how Christians are sleeping the night away. It declares the sleeping giants, a.k.a. Christians, need a *"wake up call"* to get back on the right path and answer our call to win the world to Christ.

Today, the message of this song is more relevant than ever. We need a spiritual wake up call. God is calling His church to arise and do what they are called to do. Compromise is creeping in, causing believers to lose their way. We need to *"wake up"* and get back on the right path.

I am a big believer in final words. The last words a person speaks are often what they feel is important. One of my favorite stories is about the night Thomas Jefferson and John Adams died. These two men were notorious competitors and huge rivals, and they had years of animosity between them. Adams' hatred was so strong for Jefferson, that, as he lay dying, it is said his final words were, *"Jefferson lives."* He was so put out that Jefferson outlived him, appearing to have won their feud, that he made these his final words. The irony is that, unknown to him, Jefferson had died five hours earlier!

Final words often show the heart of a man. They reflect what is most important. Jesus is one of the few people who had three final words. The first was on the cross.

Jesus said, "It is finished." With that, he bowed his head and gave up his spirit. -John 19:30 (NIV)

As he breathed his last breath, He cried out those words, **"It is finished"** (which was also the title of another POWERFUL *Petra* song). His last words on the cross were a declaration that sin had been defeated, that death was defeated, that the enemy was not victorious! God's perfect plan was taking place. These were the first last words of Jesus recorded before His death. But death couldn't hold Jesus down, and He rose again!

Unlike anyone else in history, Jesus has two more sets of final words. His final last words are in Revelations.

> ***Yes, I am coming soon. -Revelations 22:20 (NIV)***

These are Jesus' last recorded words in the Bible, but of course, they won't be His last words, because He lives forever in eternity.

In this chapter, I want to look at Jesus' second last words, the last words He spoke to His disciples before He left them and ascended to Heaven. He had risen from the dead and appeared to His disciples. Hundreds of people had seen Him alive and listened to His voice. The time had come for a final farewell to the disciples, and this is what He said:

> ***All authority in heaven and on earth has been given to me. Therefore go and make disciples of all nations, baptizing them in the name of the Father and of the Son and of the Holy Spirit, and teaching them to obey everything I have commanded you. And surely I am with you always, to the very end of the age.***
> ***-Matthew 28:18-20 (NIV)***

The Message Version says it this way:

> ***God authorized and commanded me to commission you: Go out and train everyone you meet, far and near, in this way of life, marking them by baptism in the threefold name: Father, Son, and Holy Spirit. Then instruct them in the practice of all I have commanded you. I'll be with you as you do this, day after day after day, right up to the end***

of the age.

This is the last command Jesus gave before going to Heaven with His Father: make disciples.

Win the lost.

Teach/Mentor them in My ways.

This is called the Great Commission.

Think about it: this is what Jesus felt was the most important thing to tell the disciples before He left them. They were His final thoughts. They were what He chose to emphasize. He said what He meant, and He meant what He said!

This is our calling. It is time we rise and answer the call. We must take Jesus' words seriously and put them in action! It is critical. It is urgent. We MUST do it.

WE MUST TAKE JESUS' WORDS SERIOUSLY AND PUT THEM IN ACTION!

We can't keep delaying fulfilling the Great Commission. We can't keep letting the cares of the world and the time restraints of our lives cause us to abandon the call to reach the lost.

We can't keep being so consumed with our own lives and our own struggles that we neglect reaching the lost and hurting around us. Too often in Christianity, we make it all about ourselves.

• What can God do for me?

• Why isn't He helping me?

• Why am I struggling?

• What do I need in my life?

But our salvation, while important and necessary, is not all about us! We should come to Christ, allow Him to change our lives, and then use this newfound hope and freedom to help another hurting person gain this same freedom.

THAT is what the Christian life is all about. That is fulfilling the Great Commission.

We must do it. Too much is at stake for us to ignore this call. It is life and death. What do I mean?

1. There is a hell, and good people go there.

In my opinion, we don't talk about hell enough in modern Christianity.

Hell does exist. It is a real place. The Bible makes this clear.

Jesus said that *"if your eye causes you to sin, pluck it out. It is better for you to enter the kingdom of God with one eye than to have two eyes and be thrown into hell, where 'their worm does not die, and the fire is not quenched'"* (Mark 9:47,48, NIV).

Jesus also described two men in the Bible, one went to Heaven, and another went to hell.

> *There once was a rich man, expensively dressed in the latest fashions, wasting his days in conspicuous consumption. A poor man named Lazarus, covered with sores, had been dumped on his doorstep. All he lived for was to get a meal from scraps off the rich man's table. His best friends were the dogs who came and licked his sores.*
>
> *Then he died, this poor man, and was taken up by the angels to the lap of Abraham. The rich man also died and was buried. In hell and in torment, he looked up and saw Abraham in the distance and Lazarus in his lap. He called out, 'Father Abraham, mercy! Have mercy! Send Lazarus to*

dip his finger in water to cool my tongue. I'm in agony in this fire'.

But Abraham said, 'Child, remember that in your lifetime you got the good things and Lazarus the bad things. It's not like that here. Here he's consoled and you're tormented. Besides, in all these matters there is a huge chasm set between us so that no one can go from us to you even if he wanted to, nor can anyone cross over from you to us.'
-Luke 16:19-26 MSG

These verses clearly show us there is a Heaven, and there is a hell, and the story shows one man going to Heaven, and one man going to hell.

Tragically, the church has adopted the world's view that all good people go to Heaven. Recently, a well-known superstar was in a tragic accident. This person was a good person who did good things, but they weren't a believer, and Christianity wasn't part of their lives. I wasn't surprised at all at the world declaring he was looking down on us from Heaven, but what stunned me was the number of born-again believers saying the same thing.

Now I am not saying believers should have posted that this person was in hell. Not at all! That is cruel! However, we have to realize that hell is a real place and good people who haven't accepted Christ as their Savior go there all the time. This should break our hearts and motivate us to reach the unsaved around us!

It is Biblical Truth.

For God so loved the world that he gave his one and only Son, that whoever believes in him shall not perish but have eternal life. For God did not send his Son into the world to condemn the world, but to save the world through him. Whoever believes in him is not condemned, but whoever does not believe stands condemned already because they have not believed in the name of God's one and only Son. - John 3:16-18 (NIV)

Anyone whose name was not found written in the book of life was thrown into the lake of fire. -Revelation 20:15 (NIV)

The reason so many are confused about the idea of hell is because they think of it in terms of *"good"* and *"bad."* But honestly, no one could ever be good enough to get to Heaven. That is why the only way to Heaven is through faith in Christ. There are NO good people. We are all sinners. But we receive forgiveness of sin because of Christ's death on the cross. If you accept this, ask Jesus to forgive you for your sins, and make Him your Lord and Savior, you go to Heaven. If you don't do this, you go to hell. So being good or bad has nothing to do with it. That is why we need to also know the following:

> **NO ONE COULD EVER BE GOOD ENOUGH TO GET TO HEAVEN. THAT IS WHY THE ONLY WAY TO HEAVEN IS THROUGH FAITH IN CHRIST.**

2. There is a Heaven, and bad people are there.

I love this point. Heaven has thieves, murders, criminals, abusers, and adulterers in it. Heaven is jam-packed with bad people, with sinners. How did these people get into Heaven? They realized they are sinners and turned to Christ for salvation. It is that simple.

One such person who made it into Heaven was on the cross next to Jesus.

One of the criminals hanging alongside cursed him: "Some Messiah you are! Save yourself! Save us!"

But the other one made him shut up: "Have you no fear of God? You're getting the same as him. We deserve this, but not him—he did nothing to deserve this."

Then he said, "Jesus, remember me when you enter your kingdom."

He said, "Don't worry, I will. Today you will join me in paradise."
-Luke 23:39-43 (MSG)

In 1991, the infamous murderer, pedophile, and cannibal Jeffrey Dahmer was finally arrested and sentenced to life in prison.[1] He was the worst of human beings. However, Jeffrey Dahmer found salvation in prison. He accepted Christ as his Lord and Savior. He met weekly with a Wisconsin pastor until he was murdered inside of prison. Jeffrey Dahmer is now in Heaven with Jesus. He is one example of the many *"bad"* people who are now in Heaven.

As I said, this is not an uncommon story. Heaven is filled with bad people who realized they are sinners, and turned to Christ for salvation. Do you know how a majority of these people came to this decision? Because another believer rose up, stepped into their calling, and shared the truth of the Gospel with them. They fulfilled the Great Commission!

As you see, it is vital that we all rise up and follow Jesus' commands. Every day people die and go to hell. It is heartbreaking, but true. We can stop it from happening to those around us when we share with them the truth of the Gospel, and when we offer them the same hope and freedom we have all received in our own lives.

The choice lies with each and every one of us. Will we answer the call? Will we rise to the challenge? Will we push aside complacency and step into our calling? Will we take our eyes off of ourselves and look at the hurting people around us?

It is time we rise and shine and fulfill the Great Commission. There is a lost world out there that needs the freedom, grace, mercy, and forgiveness that we have experienced through accepting Jesus as our Savior. Will you rise? Will you answer the call?

"But Jamie, I believe everything you are saying, and I want to fulfill the Great Commission, I just don't know how."

I believe it begins with a determination that we are going to rise to the occasion, step out of our comfort zone, and share our faith with others. We can't just live in complacency, ignoring our responsibility, and hoping that someone else will help people find salvation in Jesus. Instead, we need to step up and take a risk. We need to pray that the Holy Spirit will provide us with opportunities to share our faith, and then seize the moment when He opens a door.

One of the best ways to share our faith is to simply share our own story. Tell others about the difference that following Jesus has made in your life. You can prepare for this ahead of time by thinking through your story, perhaps writing it down or practice sharing it with a friend. Then, when the opportunity arises to share, you won't be scrambling for thoughts or words, but you'll be ready.

Remember, you don't have to sound *"preachy."* (In fact, it's probably better if you aren't.) Instead, just be honest, open, and dare I say *"vulnerable"*? In a conversational manner, share where you came from and the difference that Jesus made in your life. Let them know that this same hope for today and eternity is available to anyone who will admit that they are a sinner and need God's help.

Yes, I know, not everyone will want to hear it. Some will say it's not for them, and others will outright reject it. You cannot determine their choice. However, as a man of God, you are responsible to present them with the truth.

Because the Great Commission isn't an option—it's a command.

It's the responsibility of every believer. It's your mission—choose to accept it. Rise. Shine. Answer the Call.

Group Study Questions:

1. Why do you think Jesus chose to make the Great Commission His final thoughts to His followers?

2. Why is it so essential for us to fulfill the Great Commission?

3. In this chapter, we stated, *"There is a Hell, and good people go there."* What did you think about this point?

4. In this chapter, we stated, *"There is a Heaven, and bad people are there."* What did you think about this point?

5. This chapter talked about sharing your faith by sharing your story. Practice this by sharing your story with the group.

6. After reading this chapter, what is one thing you will put into practice or one thing you will change in your life?

7. How can we, as a group, help you do this?

CHAPTER THREE
YOU SNOOZE, THEY LOSE

I did it again this morning! I have been doing it for most of my life. Why can't I stop?? Why don't I have more will-power? Oh, what a wretched man I am! Why can't I gain victory?!?

What is this power it has over me?? Why can't I keep from hitting the snooze button in the morning?

Yes, I am a snooze button guy. Back in the day, I hit an actual snooze button on an alarm clock. I was late for many early morning college classes because of the snooze alarm. To this day, I occasionally have nightmares that I have to go back to college because I never graduated because I slept threw a morning class. Then I progressed from an alarm clock to a snooze on my phone alarm. Now I catch myself saying, *"Alexa, snooze"* when that brazen electronic woman dares to wake me up!

People's infatuation with the snooze alarm started in 1956 when General Electric-Telechron first marketed a Clock with a Snooze

Alarm Function.[1] It was when the glorious nine minutes of extra sleep began captivating us. It was nine minutes because the inner workings of the clock gears only allowed it to be for nine. Even now, in the digital age, alarms stick to the nine minutes, and we snooze alarmists utilize them religiously.

The snooze alarm has been the cause of many frantic mornings for millions of people worldwide. It allows us to stay comfortable in our beds for just a little longer. It doesn't really affect other people that much.

Let me ask you a question. Have you been hitting the spiritual snooze alarm? What do I mean?

In the last chapter, we discussed the need to fulfill Jesus' Great Commission. We shared how we need to reach the lost so that they experience eternity in Heaven instead of hell. Often we think we have plenty of time to reach out to those we love to share the amazing truth of Christ's redemption for our sins. We know we need to share the Gospel with them, and we have every intention of doing it... someday. The problem with this is when you snooze, they lose.

HAVE YOU BEEN HITTING THE SPIRITUAL SNOOZE ALARM?

Others hit the snooze button when they don't take action to follow God when He calls them. Way too often, I have met believers who know they have a specific call on their lives to walk a particular path. They have every intention of following God and serving Him in this calling...someday.

• Someday they will make time to take that class.

• Someday they will write that book God told them to write.

• Someday they will go on that mission's trip they are talking about going on.

- Someday they will start that men's small group.

- Someday they will beat their porn addiction.

- Someday they will gain victory over their anger issues.

They are hitting the snooze alarm on obeying God and walking in His will, thinking they have all the time in the world to do it. But we don't control time like we think we do. One day time will run out.

"Jamie, another hopeless chapter about death?"

No, not at all. I am not talking about you dying before fulfilling God's will. I am not talking about death at all. I am instead talking about our Blessed Hope.

Let's look at a parable of Jesus as we continue.

> *God's kingdom is like ten young virgins who took oil lamps and went out to greet the bridegroom. Five were silly and five were smart. The silly virgins took lamps, but no extra oil. The smart virgins took jars of oil to feed their lamps. The bridegroom didn't show up when they expected him, and they all fell asleep.*
>
> *In the middle of the night someone yelled out, 'He's here! The bride-groom's here! Go out and greet him!'*
>
> *The ten virgins got up and got their lamps ready. The silly virgins said to the smart ones, 'Our lamps are going out; lend us some of your oil.'*
>
> *They answered, 'There might not be enough to go around; go buy your own.'*
>
> *They did, but while they were out buying oil, the bridegroom arrived. When everyone who was there to greet him had gone into the wedding feast, the door was locked.*

Much later, the other virgins, the silly ones, showed up and knocked on the door, saying, 'Master, we're here. Let us in.'

He answered, 'Do I know you? I don't think I know you.'

So stay alert. You have no idea when he might arrive. - Matthew 25:1-13 (MSG)

This parable is the perfect story for this chapter. Ten women were waiting for the bridegroom to come. Five of them were ready and prepared, but five of them were hitting their spiritual snooze alarms. When the bridegroom came, five were left behind because they weren't prepared.

This passage is a parable about the rapture. The rapture, or the Blessed Hope, is a key doctrine that doesn't get discussed enough in Christianity today. I believe if we truly understood the rapture and why it is so important, a lot less compromising, procrastinating, and snooze alarm hitting would occur.

IF WE TRULY UNDERSTOOD THE RAPTURE AND WHY IT IS SO IMPORTANT, A LOT LESS COMPROMISING, PROCRASTINATING, AND SNOOZE ALARM HITTING WOULD OCCUR.

What is the rapture? The Assemblies of God 16 Fundamental Truths describe the Blessed Hope in Truth #13. It states:

The resurrection of those who have fallen asleep in Christ and their translation together with those who are alive and remain unto the coming of the Lord is the imminent and blessed hope of the church.[2]

This describes the rapture. It is an event that will happen. The Bible is clear: the rapture will take place. Only God knows the time and the hour, and we are to be ready for it at all times. As we wait for the rapture, we are to serve God and do what He called us to do.

As long as it is day, we must do the works of Him who sent me. Night is coming, when no one can work.
-John 9:4, (MSG)

God makes it clear in the Bible that the Blessed Hope is a rallying cry to action, not a reason to hit the snooze button. In 1 Thessalonians, Paul told the church about the rapture and how it comes like a thief in the night. Well, after they read this letter, they figured it was going to happen soon, so why should they go to work, why reach out to the lost, why do anything? When Paul heard this, he wrote them another letter telling them to get back to work, get back to life, and return to ministry. The same goes for us.

We don't know when the rapture will happen; only God does. This is important to remember:

Above all, you must understand that in the last days scoffers will come, scoffing and following their own evil desires. They will say, "Where is this 'coming' he promised? Ever since our ancestors died, everything goes on as it has since the beginning of creation." -2 Peter 3:3-4, (NIV)

God has chosen not to tell us when the rapture will happen so that we stay focused and run the race He has called us to run. He also does it out of infinite grace, delaying it so even more people come to salvation and repentance.

The Lord is not slow in keeping his promise, as some understand slowness. Instead, He is patient with you, not wanting anyone to perish, but everyone to come to repentance. -2 Peter 3:9, (NIV)

But guys, it will happen. The rapture will come. Paul tells us exactly what will happen.

For the Lord himself will come down from heaven, with a loud command, with the voice of the archangel and with

the trumpet call of God, and the dead in Christ will rise first. After that, we who are still alive and are left will be caught up together with them in the clouds to meet the Lord in the air. And so we will be with the Lord forever.
-1 Thessalonians 4:16-17, (NIV)

Someday a trumpet is gonna blow. What will it sound like? I have no idea, but when I imagine it, the closest thing I can think of is the Rocky movies. Whenever Rocky is in a fight, he gets beat up, but then you hear the trumpets, *"Ba bum bum ba bum"* and you know Rocky is making his comeback. Every day, we are getting attacked, we face trials and opposition, but one day those trumpets will blow, and away we go!! We will literally fly to meet Jesus in the clouds. How cool will that be!

But let me tell you something wonderful, a mystery I'll probably never fully understand. We're not all going to die—but we are all going to be changed. You hear a blast to end all blasts from a trumpet, and in the time that you look up and blink your eyes—it's over. On signal from that trumpet from heaven, the dead will be up and out of their graves, beyond the reach of death, never to die again. At the same moment and in the same way, we'll all be changed. In the resurrection scheme of things, this has to happen: everything perishable taken off the shelves and replaced by the imperishable, this mortal replaced by the immortal. Then the saying will come true:

Death swallowed by triumphant Life! Who got the last word, oh, Death? Oh, Death, who's afraid of you now? -1 Corinthians 15:51-55, (MSG)

We get a new body!! Goodbye limp, goodbye stabbing pain in my foot, goodbye shriveled hands, goodbye bad back. I can't wait! We will all say goodbye to all our physical limitations, and, even more importantly, goodbye to our mortal, sinful body. Hello glorified state in Heaven with Jesus! I can't wait!!!

It is going to be great for all those who are raptured. But what about those who are left behind? What happens to those who don't make it in the rapture?

Sadly, they are left to experience literal hell on earth. Have you ever read all of the nightmares in the book of Revelation? All of that is known as the Great Tribulation, and it is ushered in by the rapture. Our Blessed Hope is that God rescues us and saves us from living through the tribulation horrors. We are safely in Heaven with Jesus while the earth is in utter hell.

The Assemblies of God Position Paper on the Rapture of the Church confirms that the tribulation follows the rapture. It states:

"It is consistent with God's dealings with His people in the Old Testament to believe that the Church will be removed from the world before the Great Tribulation. God did not send the Flood until Noah and his family were safe in the ark. He did not destroy Sodom until Lot was taken out."[3]

THAT is why we cannot keep hitting our spiritual snooze button. I, for one, do not want to be here for the Great Tribulation. I want to fly away when I hear that trumpet blow! We need to stay on fire for God. We need to go where He leads us. We need to walk in complete obedience and do what He calls us to do. We need to remove compromise in our lives and pursue holiness. We need to follow God wholeheartedly without abandon, and run after everything He has called us to do.

We must also work hard to help other people we know and love to come to Christ. We need to share the Gospel with them. Our desire needs to be God's desire that ***"not wanting anyone to perish, but everyone to come to repentance" (2 Peter 3:9, NIV)***

We should do all we can to make sure that:

- Our brother doesn't have to choose to take the mark of the beast or follow God to his death.

- Our sister doesn't face martyrdom because she fooled around with her Christianity, got left behind, and decided to follow Christ during the tribulation.

- Our best friend isn't devoured by fire when the sun melts parts of the earth. (Rev. 16:8-9)

- Our co-worker isn't forced to suit up and fight in the battle of Armageddon.

These things will take place. People will experience them. The good news is God's grace and salvation will still be available to those left behind. They will die for choosing God, but they can be saved and go to Heaven. But we can spare them this brutal death and everything they experience in the tribulation leading up to their martyrdom. We can share the Gospel with them and help ensure that when we fly away, they do, too!

Guys, it is so essential for us to rise and shine. It is literally life and death. We need to stop hitting the spiritual snooze alarm. We have to follow God with complete abandon, walking in obedience. Then we need to share the truth of our freedom and victory with the lost. There is no time to spare. Maybe there is a tomorrow, or maybe that Rocky trumpet blares tonight.

This topic is so important. You need to ask yourself some critical questions:

- Am I walking in complete obedience to God?

- Have I delayed doing anything God has asked me to do?

- Have I been ignoring areas of sin or compromise in my life?

- Have I faced struggles and strongholds and worked to gain the victory?

- Is there anyone with whom I have delayed sharing the truth of the Gospel?

- If the rapture happened tonight, am I ready? Are those around me ready?

These are hard questions, but we must ask ourselves. We hate to look at them, but they are way easier than being left behind and facing the tribulation. Are you ready? Are those you love ready? It is time to rise and shine.

Group Study Questions:

1. Have you been using the *"someday"* excuse? What is your *"someday"* that you have been putting off?

2. Are you walking in complete obedience to God?

3. Have you delayed doing anything God has asked you to do?

4. Have you been ignoring areas of sin or compromise in your life?

5. Have you faced struggles and strongholds and worked to gain the victory?

6. Is there anyone with whom you have delayed sharing the truth of the Gospel?

7. If the rapture happened tonight, are you ready? Are those around you ready?

8. After reading this chapter, what is one thing you will put into practice or one thing you will change in your life?

9. How can we, as a group, help you do this?

CHAPTER FOUR
STAYING UP

Did you ever wake up earlier than you wanted? Maybe you're noisy neighbor woke you up while he hammered away at his new deck project or a car backfired as its owner peeled out of the driveway. Perhaps your bladder woke you up (hey, the older you get, the more it happens).

Whatever the reason, many times we wake up earlier than we had planned. I know I have. Sometimes I just get an earlier start to the day. Other times, I will lay in bed and pray. However, sometimes I do something really stupid. I lay there for awhile and fall back asleep.

If you have ever done this, you know what happens next. It is twice as hard to wake up again. You feel tired and groggy all day. Falling back into bed makes getting back up so difficult! The same is true in our spiritual lives.

I have seen it so often. Men decide to rise and shine. They decide to get up and commit themselves to follow God wholeheartedly. Then the enemy throws a temptation at us, and we spiritually fall back into bed. We fall back into a sin pattern. We do that thing we vowed not to do anymore. We get knocked down, and we feel like it is impossible to get back up.

You vow never to look at porn again. Then you see something that excites you, and before you know it, you're on your computer doing the very thing you said you wouldn't do.

You promise yourself and God you won't be an abusive man anymore. Then you have a rough day, you get home tired, and your wife and kids immediately come to you with 1,000 problems all at once, and you lose your temper.

You commit yourself to cut all lies and deceit out of your life, but then you are confronted with a mistake or error, and you go to your old standby of lie and deny.

YOU CAN GET BACK UP. YOU CAN GAIN VICTORY!

The list of ways we fall goes on and on. As soon as we fall, we get visited by shame and defeat telling us that we can't get back up. We can't try again. They tell us we will never be able to gain victory, so why should we even bother?

Eventually, you find yourself back in your spiritual bed with the covers pulled up tight, feeling lost, alone, and hopeless. You see no way back out of bed and onto your feet. You think there is no chance you can ever gain victory.

Guys, this is a lie from the enemy to keep you defeated. You can get back up. You can gain victory!

Because of Christ's death on the cross, we have freedom from sin. We are declared righteous.

> *God made him who had no sin to be sin for us, so that in him we might become the righteousness of God.*
> *-2 Corinthians 5:21 (NIV)*

We are righteous because of Christ's death on the cross. When we confess our sins to God, He gives us the grace and forgiveness we need. He declares us innocent of our sins. God gives us grace and forgiveness. He loves us and doesn't condemn us when we come to Him in repentance.

> *As a father has compassion on his children, so the Lord has compassion on those who fear him;*
> *-Psalms 103:13 (NIV)*

He is your Heavenly Father. He treats you the way a good father treats his kid. When your child messes up or does something wrong, if they come to you and confess, you don't treat them poorly or disown them. You don't tell them to get out of your sight. You don't tell them there is no recovery from their actions. No, you forgive them, you let them know how much you love them, and that no actions they could ever do would make you stop loving them.

More than likely, you lovingly punish them. You help them face the consequences of their actions and stand by them as they walk forward. You help them get back up and move forward.

"But Jamie, I asked God to forgive me and save me from my sins. But then I sinned again and fell back into the trap."

I understand that. But you can't stay down. You need to get back up!

> *...for though the righteous fall seven times, they rise again... -Proverbs 24:16 (NIV)*

Get back up! When the righteous man falls, he gets back up. When the enemy throws a punch, and it lands, you pick yourself off of the mat.

This verse makes me think of one of my favorite movie franchises…Rocky. Ever Rocky movie shows one scene that is the same. In every fight, we see Rocky getting beat to a pulp. He takes blow after blow as his face is bleeding and swollen. Then we see the blow that knocks him to the mat. But then what happens? He gets back up!

In every movie, we see Rocky slowly rise off the mat and get back to his feet to fight. Apollo Creed, Clubber Lang, Ivan Drago, and Mason Dixon all look on in disbelief as Rocky gets back up from the beating they give to him.

My favorite example of this is from the latest Rocky films, the Creed franchise.[1] The example I want to discuss is in *Creed 2*. This expansion of the Rocky franchise picks up with Adonis Creed, coached by Rocky Balboa, winning the heavyweight title. But then he faces a challenge from both his and Rocky's past when Ivan Drago's son challenges Creed to a fight.

Remember, Ivan Drago killed Apollo Creed in the ring. Now his son was challenging Donny. Adonis takes the fight and gets beaten to a pulp. It's bad, and he spends weeks in the hospital. He is wounded, but even worse, his spirit is crushed.

After the loss, Donny kind of crawls back into bed. He won't fight; he won't train. But eventually, Rocky gets through to him, and Donny agrees to a rematch. After one of the most epic training montages in a Rocky movie, Adonis is ready and enters the ring for a rematch. It goes well for him through the first few rounds, but the fight turns around in round 9, and Donny starts getting beat again.

Viktor Drago lands blow after blow against Donny, and he

eventually gives him the roundhouse that sends Donny to the mat. Donny is down, and he looks to be out. As he struggles to get back to his feet, he sees his wife and mom yelling for him to get up. He sees Rocky say, *"Get up, kid."* He looks around, weak, and unable to stand.

But then we see something inside of him change. He punches the mat, first one fist and then the other. He repeatedly hits the mat. At that moment, he gets mad! He gets tired of being knocked down. He gets angry at feeling weak and defeated. He punches the mat, and he stands to his feet.

He got back up. Drago looks at him in stunned disbelief that he got back up after such a beating! Donny went at Drago with every ounce of strength and determination he had, and he eventually knocks him down and wins the fight.

Donny had to make a choice. Was he going to stay down on the mat defeated, or was he going to get back up and fight?

GET UP OFF THE MAT!

Guys, you are down on the mat. The enemy has knocked you down over and over. For some of you, it was a recent defeat. For others, you have been down and out for weeks, months, even years. Like Adonis, you are beaten, bleeding spiritually, and you don't know what to do. It is time for you to get angry. Punch the mat, get mad at your current state, and find the resolve to fight. Get up off the mat!

Adonis looked around at his family for encouragement. They all said, *"Get up!"* Guys, you have family and friends all around you who want to see you crawl out of bed and get back up. They want you to gain victory. They want you to get up. You need to punch that mat, resolve to get up, and fight.

In the movie, when Donny got up, the ref asked him his name, and he yelled, *"Creed."* The enemy is going to ask you who you think you are. Why do you think you can fight? Who do you think you are to get back up and face off again?

When you hear these questions or have these thoughts, you need to answer by screaming, *"I am a child of GOD!"*

You have everything you need to rise off your knees, wipe the blood off your chin, sweat off your brow, and get back into the fight. Are you ready to punch the mat and get back up?

"The righteous man falls seven times, but he gets back up."

Don't let yourself fall prey to the enemy's lies that you are hopeless, that you can never gain victory. He is a liar! John 8:44 says he is the father of lies.

STOP BELIEVING HIM!

Grace, forgiveness, and victory await you from your Heavenly Father. He does not condemn you; He forgives. You may need to face the consequences of your sin, but He will walk with you as you deal with the results. He is your loving Father Who wants to see you gain victory.

> **GRACE, FORGIVENESS, AND VICTORY AWAIT YOU FROM YOUR HEAVENLY FATHER. HE DOES NOT CONDEMN YOU; HE FORGIVES.**

You have been in bed for too long. Your sin has knocked you back into bed, and you stayed there for too long. It seems impossible to get up and start again. You feel there is no point; you will just end up back where you are now. But it is time to get up!

In the next chapter, we will look at steps you can take to walk in freedom once you are back on your feet, but I don't want to rush past this moment.

Do you find yourself knocked back down because you have fallen back into an old sin or an old pattern? Do you feel like you have no hope and no way back? Is shame punching you over and over again?

If that is you, take this chapter seriously. Choose today to get angry with the sin. Despise it. Want nothing to do with it! Punch the mattress, get back up out of bed, and get back into action.

Here's a couple of suggestions to help you get back up.

First, tell a godly man you trust (a reliable person, not the church gossip) about your struggle and decision to get back up. It will help you to speak it, and he'll hold you accountable. When you struggle, he'll be there cheering for you.

Second, develop a game plan to help you avoid getting knocked back down. We will help you with this in the next chapter, but for more in-depth help, buy and read Mantour Ministries' book, *"Whatever It Takes."* This book is ridiculously practical. It gives you a game plan for how to keep your commitment. That's why we wrote it —so that you have something to take home and help you endure the fight.

Finally, remember that I believe you can do it. I am in your corner. Like Rocky, I am standing in your corner, saying, *"Get up, Kid!"* I know you have everything you need to rise. I believe you have the strength and endurance to start again. It is time to kick off those sheets and get back up. Do it today.

Group Study Questions:

1. Are you now or have you ever struggled with getting back up after a spiritual defeat?

2. Do you struggle with seeing God as a loving Father? Why?

3. What will it take for you to finally get angry at being down on the mat?

4. What steps can you take to get back up?

5. Do you want to get back up? Or are you content to stay down and defeated?

6. After reading this chapter, what is one thing you will put into practice or one thing you will change in your life?

7. How can we, as a group, help you do this?

CHAPTER FIVE
GETTING DRESSED PART 1

I am very proud to announce that I have showered and gotten dressed every day this year!

"Good for you Jamie, but aren't you setting the bar pretty low there?"

Yeah, I can see why the reader of that first sentence would think this. But to understand it, you have to know that I am writing this book in the middle of the 2020 Covid-19 lockdown. During this time, when we were all locked away in our homes, unable to leave our house, and unlikely to see other people, so many have abandoned things like showering and clothes. It stunned me the number of people who stayed in their pajamas all day or openly admitted to not regularly showering.

I made it my goal not to fall into this pattern. Quarantine life was hard enough without sitting in my own filth and wearing the same Batman pajamas for days. Getting up and dressing each day makes me feel clean. It gives a definitive breaking point so that I keep my days straight, and gives me a sense of purpose and control. It provides a sense of routine to the day, a starting point.

I believe that spiritually we also need to rise and get dressed every day. As a matter of fact, the Bible tells us this, and it even tells us what to wear.

> *Finally, be strong in the Lord and in His mighty power. Put on the full armor of God, so that you can take your stand against the devil's schemes.*
> *-Ephesians 6:10-11 (NIV)*

In this Scripture, Paul tells us that each day we are to *"Put on"* the full armor of God so that we can stand against the devil's evil schemes. What exactly does this mean, and how can we practically apply it to our lives?

THERE IS A CONSTANT AND ONGOING BATTLE BETWEEN THE FORCES OF GOOD AND EVIL IN THE SPIRIT WORLD—GOD'S KINGDOM AND SATAN'S KINGDOM.

Reality is that there is more to this world than the tangible things that we can see, hear, touch, smell, and taste. These things belong to the physical world. However, beyond that world is the spiritual world. There is a constant and ongoing battle between the forces of good and evil in the spirit world—God's kingdom and Satan's kingdom.

As Ephesians 6:12 says, *'For our struggle is not against flesh and blood, but against the rulers, against the authorities, against the powers of this dark world and against the spiritual forces of evil in the heavenly realms.' (NIV)*

You cannot say that you believe in the Bible and not believe in spiritual warfare. It's impossible.

The fact that there is a war between God's kingdom and Satan's kingdom is a fundamental truth of the Bible. We have an enemy who **HATES** us and wants to utterly **DESTROY** us. If he has to spend an eternity in Hell, he wants to bring as many of us with him as possible. We are born as sinners in his kingdom, but when we accept God's offer of salvation and reconciliation, we leave the kingdom of darkness and enter the kingdom of light. The enemy sees this as treason against him, and he wants to destroy you.

Every book of the New Testament mentions demons, evil angels, or Satan. If you claim to be a Christian who believes the Bible is the Word of God, you must accept the fact that the war between God's kingdom and Satan's kingdom exists. You must also accept that you are a part of that battle.

Here's where it gets murky. You see, there are many Christians who don't want to be in a battle. Spiritually, they are pacifists. They are Switzerland. They don't like war, and they don't want to participate. Unfortunately, the enemy, Satan, has deceived them into thinking that they have an option. However, nothing is further from the truth.

The truth is that no human being can choose whether or not they are involved in the spiritual war. If you are a human being with an eternal soul, there is a battle raging for your soul and your eternal destiny. Just like a baby born in Israel doesn't choose whether they want to be in a war with the surrounding countries, you don't get to decide whether or not you are in a war. An Israeli baby is born into a war zone. Even before he's taken his first steps or spoken his first word, he has enemies that hate him. He doesn't get a choice. It's a fact of his life.

In the same way, every human being is born into a spiritual war zone. We don't get to choose whether or not we are in a spiritual battle. The fact is that we are. The only two choices that you have are:

1. Are you on God's side or Satan's side?

2. Are you going to *"put on"* the weapons God has given you to fight and gain victory, or are you going to run around the spiritual battlefield naked and unprotected?

Let's assume that anyone who is reading this chapter has chosen to be on God's side. You made that decision when you accepted Jesus as your personal Savior and became a Christian. At that point, you transferred your allegiance from the kingdom of Satan to the kingdom of God.

Having made that decision, Satan now sees you as a traitor, and he hates you. Anyone who has accepted Jesus as their Savior and joined God's army is on the enemy's hit list. He wants nothing more than to destroy your life, your relationship with God, your family, your testimony, and your reputation. He will use every weapon at his disposal to try to destroy you.

The good news is that *"the One Who is in you (Jesus) is greater than the one who is in the world (Satan)."* -I John 4:4 (NIV)

Isaiah 54:17 says, *"No weapon forged against you will prevail,"*. (NIV)

Ultimately, God is in control of the universe. He is far more powerful than Satan. As we see in the first chapter of Job, Satan can only wage war against people to the point that God allows it. Because of this, we do not have to be afraid.

> *For God has not given us a spirit of fear, but of power and of love and of a sound mind. -2 Timothy 1:7 (NKJV)*

Still, one truth that Christians need to accept is that God will allow Satan to attack Christians so that Christians will learn to fight. Through these battles, we will mature spiritually, grow deeper in our relationship with God, and win other people to Christ.

As 1 Peter 1:7 says, *"These have come so that the proven genuineness of your faith—of greater worth than gold, which perishes even though refined by fire—may result in praise, glory and honor when Jesus Christ is revealed." (NIV)*

In short, God allows the battle for our good so that we will be conformed to the image of His Son, recognize we are nothing without Him, and be prepared for eternity. Even though God could remove all battles from our lives, He won't. He wants us to learn to fight.

So that's the reality of the situation:

There is a spiritual battle. We're in it.

Satan, our enemy hates us and wants to use all means possible to destroy us.

God will allow these attacks and battles to come our way so that we grow spiritually.

This brings us to our second choice, *Are you going to choose to "put on" the spiritual armor that God has given you, or are you going to be a wimpy, defeated victim that falls into every trap the enemy sets for you?*

This is where the rubber meets the road.

When we choose not to wear our spiritual armor and use the weapons God has given us to live in victory, when we choose to ignore the fact that there is a spiritual war going on around us, we are choosing to lose the battle.

Worse yet, when we choose to believe that there is no spiritual battle, thus there's no need for us to *"put on"* the armor of God, we are disobeying God and the Bible. As Christians, we aren't given the option of whether or not to use our spiritual weapons and fight. No, if we continue reading on in Ephesians 6:13-17 we read:

> *Put on the full armor of God, so that when the day of evil comes, you may be able to stand your ground, and after you have done everything, to stand. Stand firm then, with the belt of truth buckled around your waist, with the breastplate of righteousness in place, and with your feet fitted with the readiness that comes from the gospel of peace. In addition to all this, take up the shield of faith, with which you can extinguish all the flaming arrows of the evil one. Take the helmet of salvation and the sword of the Spirit, which is the Word of God. (NIV)*

Not one sentence in that verse says, "*If you want to*" or "*If you feel like it*." These are imperative sentences commanding us to use these weapons to win the spiritual battles in our lives.

Failure to do it will bring defeat. Obedience to God's command to dress will bring victory. It's that simple. As men of God, our passionate pursuit is to walk in God's total victory.

AS MEN OF GOD, OUR PASSIONATE PURSUIT IS TO WALK IN GOD'S TOTAL VICTORY.

Many of you may recall the old story, "*The Emperor's New Clothes*" by Hans Christian Andersen.[1] If you've never heard the story, it's the tale of a very vain emperor obsessed with wearing the latest, most fashionable clothes. Everyone in the kingdom knew that he wasted all of his time and money on such endeavors.

Then one day a group of swindlers and con men entered the kingdom and approached the king with the proposition that they could make him the finest suit of clothes ever—the only catch was that the suit was to be made of a fabric that was invisible to anyone who is unfit for his position or *"hopelessly stupid."*

Of course, the king agreed, but the problem was that as the swindlers went through the motions of designing, measuring, and creating the new suit of clothes, the king couldn't see them. Not wanting to admit that he may be unfit for his positions, stupid, or incompetent, the king plays along, as do all of his noblemen. In fact, everyone in the kingdom goes along with the charade and pretends that the king is wearing a beautiful suit of clothes even though it was apparent to everyone that the king was buck naked---and making an appearance in a parade none the less!

Throughout the whole kingdom, there was only one child that didn't get the memo to *"pretend the king is wearing clothes even though he isn't."* Not knowing any better, the child cried out, *"The emperor is naked!"* Soon everyone began to murmur the same thing and very soon all shouted, *"The emperor is not wearing anything!"*

Finally, the story ends with the saddest line of all: *"The emperor realized the truth but preferred to believe that his people were stupid."* 2

What does this have to do with spiritually dressing?

Basically this…I believe it's time that each of us examined our hearts and asked ourselves the question, *"Am I really putting on the spiritual weapons God has provided? Am I imitating the stupid emperor and pretending to be wearing a suit while I'm really running around spiritually naked?"*

Here's a tip: The enemy of our souls knows the truth. He's going to attack us in every area that we've left spiritually vulnerable. The only way to combat his attacks is to really and truly apply the principles about the Armor of God to our lives each and every day.

Of course, the choice is yours.

When the answers to the above questions reveal obvious gaps in your armor, will you choose to make the lifestyle changes to wear the full Armor of God, or will you, like the emperor, choose to ignore the truth and remain spiritually naked?

You see, the question isn't *"Are the clothes provided?"*

We've already established that God has given us everything we need to take your stand against the enemy's evil schemes.

The question is: *"Will you choose to take your spiritual clothes out of the closet and put them on?"*

Will you rise and get dressed so you can then shine bright to the world?

In the next chapter, we will dive deeper into exactly what each item of clothing is we are to put on. Still, before we do that, we need to do spiritually what I decided to do physically in the middle of the coronavirus pandemic...commit to rising every day and getting dressed.

Will you commit yourself to daily putting on and living in your spiritual armor? Will you rise and become a warrior for God, or will you stay in your filth and grime and let the enemy walk all over you?

Only you can decide! If you choose to get dressed, let's move into chapter six and look at our wardrobe.

Group Study Questions:

1. Do you believe in spiritual warfare? Why or why not?

2. In this chapter, we stated, *"The only two choices that you have are: 'Are you on God's side or Satan's side?' and 'Are you going to 'put on' the weapons God has given you to fight and gain victory, or are you going to run around the spiritual battlefield naked and unprotected?'"* Which choice will you make?

3. In this chapter, we stated, *"As men of God, our passionate pursuit is to walk in God's total victory."* What does this mean, and how can you do it?

4. Will you choose to take your spiritual clothes out of the closet and put them on? Will you rise and get dressed so you can then shine bright to the world?

5. After reading this chapter, what is one thing you will put into practice or one thing you will change in your life?

6. How can we, as a group, help you do this?

CHAPTER SIX
GETTING DRESSED PART 2

As a guy, I have to admit I don't really put that much thought into what I am going to wear. I just get up and put on what is best suited for my day. When I am at home writing, I wear some sweatpants and a t-shirt. If it is a Mantour day, jeans and a Mantour shirt. If I am speaking on a Sunday, a pair of nice dress pants and a dress shirt. On game day, my Broncos Jersey!

Women put a lot more thought into what they wear. Men have clothes; women have wardrobes. How many times have you seen a woman stand in front of a full closet and say, *"I have nothing to wear"*? A wise man just slowly backs out of the room, a foolish man says, *"You have loads of clothes, just pick something!"*

Did you know you have a spiritual wardrobe? Paul tells us what our spiritual closet contains.

> *...Put on the full armor of God, so that when the day of evil comes, you may be able to stand your ground, and after*

you have done everything, to stand.

Stand firm then, with the belt of truth buckled around your waist, with the breastplate of righteousness in place, and with your feet fitted with the readiness that comes from the gospel of peace. In addition to all this, take up the shield of faith, with which you can extinguish all the flaming arrows of the evil one. Take the helmet of salvation and the sword of the Spirit, which is the word of God.

And pray in the Spirit on all occasions with all kinds of prayers and requests. With this in mind, be alert and always keep on praying for all the Lord's people. - Ephesians 6:13-18 (NIV)

That's your spiritual wardrobe.

For many years, there was a teaching in the church that all you had to do was get up every morning and read this Scripture saying, *"I choose to put on the belt of truth, the helmet of salvation, etc..."* As you got dressed, you would be choosing to put on the armor of God as well.

Although I'm not criticizing this practice, I've done it; it still seems like there has to be more to it. I'm sure the Apostle Paul intended more than just reciting a few words each morning. Practically applying this principle must involve a change of heart and the choice to make these spiritual virtues a part of our life, wearing them just as we wear a suit of clothes each day.

So what does each article of clothing mean for us? Let's look at each one.

1. Belt of truth

Why is it so important that we put on truth every day?

Well, truth is the foundational garment that holds everything else in its proper place. Truth is consistent---it never changes. Therefore, it has a stabilizing effect on our lives. Like a buckle holds up our pants, truth puts and keeps everything in its proper place.

When we live in truth, we will live in freedom. As John 8:32 says, *"Then you will know the truth, and the truth will set you free." (NIV)*

If you want to live a life free from the bondage of sin, you have to *"put on truth."*

TRUTH IS CONSISTENT---IT NEVER CHANGES.

If you want peace and stability in your life, rather than being tossed along by every new idea, emotion, or fad that comes along, you need to choose to *"put on truth."*

Ultimately, if you want to successfully overcome the spiritual attacks of the enemy on your life, you've got to start with the foundation of choosing to live each day, walking in, believing, and wearing truth.

This is not easy. Everywhere we look, lies surround us. Each day, so many of the entertainment outlets available to us speak lies in our minds about what is right and what is wrong, acceptable, and unacceptable. Constantly, we are lied to about what is normal, healthy, and socially acceptable. Even within some churches, we are told to compromise our moral standards in the spirit of tolerance.

However, there are absolutes.

There is only One True God Who created the world and is still in control of it.

He sent His One and Only Son, Jesus, to die on the cross and redeem mankind from their sins. He is the One and Only Way, the Truth, and the Life.

The Bible is God's Word. It speaks the ultimate truth. Within its pages, sin is clearly defined. So is the path to salvation. Those who choose to accept Jesus as their Savior will spend eternity with Him. Those who reject Him will spend eternity in Hell. Although this may sound harsh, it is real.

As Christians, we need to keep these fundamental truths of our faith in the forefront of our minds, and not allow ourselves to be deceived by the lies of a culture telling us otherwise. When we lose sight of these truths and let lies put us into a state of spiritual anesthesia, we lose the very essence of who we are as Christians. We stop being light in a dark world because we're more comfortable blending in with the world.

These truths are the basis for our life, and they define our purpose and our calling on this earth. They are what drive us to abandon ourselves, follow God wholeheartedly, and do our part to fulfill the Great Commission. No wonder our enemy is working overtime, trying to get us to replace these truths with lies! It is up to us to choose whether we will believe lies or truth.

2. Breastplate of righteousness

What is a breastplate?

When I think of a breastplate, I think of a baseball catcher. Part of a catcher's equipment is a padded vest that covers his chest. It protects him. It keeps a 100 mph fastball from hitting his bare chest, which could do tremendous damage to his organs, especially his heart.

A breastplate did the same thing for a soldier. It was a steel covering that protected the chest, keeping safe vital organs like the heart, lungs, and kidneys. It kept an arrow, spear, or sword from penetrating the heart.

It is important for a man of God to protect their heart. The book of Proverbs emphasizes why we must protect our hearts.

> *Above all else, guard your heart, for everything you do flows from it. -Proverbs 4:23 (NIV)*

We need to protect our hearts. But why with righteousness? Righteousness simply means being or doing what is right. You live your life with integrity. We live a pure and holy life.

We need to put on right living. We were declared righteous before God the moment we are saved. But it is our job to continue living a holy and righteous life. We need to make sure we guard our heart by watching what we allow to influence our heart. We must not allow the wrong people, the wrong viewing habits, the wrong speech habits, the wrong actions, anything contrary to the Word of God, to settle into our hearts and cause us to fall into temptation or sin. We wear a righteous lifestyle to guard our hearts and keep it pure and holy before God.

3. Shoes of Peace

I don't know about you, but I have several people in my life who are always trying to steal my peace. They are constantly trying to stir things up and create conflict or a point of tension because that's where they are comfortable.

These *"Karens"* run on the adrenaline that comes with drama. It's like a drug to them. Needing the rush they get from it, they tend to create drama in every situation in life.

I find myself encountering people like this all the time. If you think about it, I'd be willing to bet that you're familiar with these people.

How do I know? Unfortunately, there are far too many people who struggle with issues from their past that cause them to consciously or unconsciously respond to life's circumstances in chaos and conflict, drama, and division. Like a magnet, they draw confusion to themselves. Like a super-powered vacuum, they try to suck everyone around them into their melodrama, eliminating peace.

If you've ever experienced this, you know what I'm describing. You're probably picturing someone in your mind that continually seems to be trying to involve you in their latest drama or conflict. You might even be wondering, *"How can I keep myself from constantly being sucked in, losing my peace, and having their drama control my life?"*

You put on the sandals of peace.

In his book, *"Victory in Spiritual Warfare,"* Dr. Tony Evans gives us a good picture of what Paul meant when he describes the ancient soldier's shoes of peace. He shares that Roman sandals were sandals that had nails sticking out of the bottom to give them traction and help them keep their footing. This traction kept the soldier from slipping and sliding, much like cleats help a football player today. It gave him sure footing, making mobility in battle easier while also making it more difficult to be knocked down. [1]

So when Paul instructs you to have your feet *"shod,"* he is talking about getting firm footing so that the enemy, Satan, can't knock you off your feet. You can *"stand firm"* because the cleats coming out of your sneakers have dug deep into the solid ground beneath you.

How do you stand your ground when someone tries to steal your peace, draw you into a conflict, or fill a situation with drama and confusion?

You recognize that you're fighting a spiritual battle and choose to put on your shoes of peace that are armed with super-strong cleats to help you stand firm as you say, *"No, I'm not being sucked in---I'm going to stand in peace and walk in peace."*

When your friend comes to you with all the latest gossip, trying to draw you into conflict, you choose to walk in peace and say, *"I'm not choosing sides, I'm not getting involved, go and settle this the way the Bible says you should."*

When someone is provoking you (probably on Facebook lol), trying to start a fight and make you lose your peace, you can choose to strap on your shoes of peace and tell yourself, *"This is not worth fighting about; I'm not going to be sucked into a battle and lose my peace."*

In this case, I'm talking about minor annoyances, personality conflicts, and things like that. I understand that there are times when you have to take a stand for right against the forces of wrong. However, I've been learning to take a step back and access a skirmish before losing my peace. I find myself asking, *"Will this battle reap eternal consequences?"* If someone's soul is in danger, a battle needs to be fought. If I'm simply annoyed or responding to a provocation, I need to refrain and choose to walk in peace.

You see, what I'm realizing is that we often allow our peace to be stolen simply because we do not recognize that we're fighting a spiritual battle. Because we think we're just dealing with difficult situations or difficult people, we don't make a choice to put on our spiritual shoes and walk in peace. Even though we have this powerful weapon of defense at our disposal, we choose not to put it on---then we wonder why we're always defeated. The real benefit comes as we make the conscious choice to wear these character traits and allow them to influence our behavior in each area of our lives.

When you start using peace as a defensive weapon, you'll find that you won't be caught up in every wind of chaos and confusion that comes along. Instead, your shoes of peace will help you stand firm and victorious in any battle, unable to be defeated or shaken.

4. Shield of Faith

So what does it mean to *"have faith"*?

Hebrews 11:6 gives us a pretty accurate definition.

> ***And without faith it is impossible to please God, because anyone who comes to Him must believe that He exists and that He rewards those who earnestly seek Him. (NIV)***

Looking at this verse, we see that the #1 ingredient in an accurate definition of faith is: Believing that God exists and that He is Who He claims to be in the Bible.

> ***In addition to all this, take up the shield of faith, with which you can extinguish all the 'flaming arrows of the evil one.'***

To really understand this verse, we need to know more about two things: fiery darts and shields. (Because let's face it: we don't see a lot of either in our day to day lives.)

So what are fiery darts?

Have you ever seen *"Robin Hood Men in Tights"*?[2] This hilarious movie opens up with soldiers shooting flaming arrows in the opening credits. The arrows fly through the air, followed by the names of the director, producer, etc., and then they land on the roofs of the villagers, burning their houses. It is hilarious as the villagers say, *"Every time there is a new Robin Hood Movie, they burn down our house!"*

A fiery dart is a flaming arrow. Every day, the enemy of our souls sends lies and doubts about God, about Christianity, and about the need to live for Jesus toward our mind. How do we stop these arrows? We use our shield of faith.

What does a shield do? Well, in this verse, the shield described is a large Roman shield covered in leather or some kind of animal skin. The soldier would then dip the shield in water so that if a fiery arrow came at him, it would be instantly snuffed out.

In our lives, faith is the dripping wet shield that instantly extinguishes the flaming arrows of the enemy. When the enemy attacks us with lies or doubt, we have faith that God will do what He said He would do. He promises us victory. He says there is always a way out. He told us that we could trust Him to be there with us and lead us through. Faith guards our hearts and helps us gain victory.

> **WHEN THE ENEMY ATTACKS US WITH LIES OR DOUBT, WE HAVE FAITH THAT GOD WILL DO WHAT HE SAID HE WOULD DO.**

5. Helmet of Salvation

How do we choose to *"Take Up the Helmet of Salvation"* as Paul tells us in Ephesians 6:17? The first thing we need to understand is that we *"take up"* or *"put on"* the helmet of salvation by choosing to give salvation control of our lives and allow it to dominate our minds.

For example, we've already talked about the fact that salvation provides us with forgiveness and deliverance from sin. Once we have asked Jesus into our hearts, we are forgiven.

Knowing the awesomeness of this fact should make us extremely grateful. Remember, forgiveness is not something we deserve. It isn't something you're entitled to receive. In fact, quite the contrary, there's absolutely no way you could ever earn a gift this tremendous. In light of this knowledge, every Christian should be so intensely grateful to God that they want to live every part of their lives for Jesus, giving themselves to Him 100% wholeheartedly.

This knowledge of what it means to be forgiven and made right with God should cover our heads like a helmet. Every thought, every action, every emotion, and every behavior should have to pass through the filter of *"Because I have received salvation through Christ, I will think or do...."* If we truly applied this vital piece of equipment to our lives, we would no longer be dabbling with the sin or doubts that leave us open to the enemy's spiritual attacks. Instead, the knowledge of our salvation would protect us.

Another way that acting on the knowledge of what salvation provides can protect us is by realizing that salvation gives us deliverance from sin. Because of the victory that Jesus won at the cross, Christians do not have to live their lives controlled by any demonic powers or strongholds, generational iniquities, or demonic oppressions from the sins we've committed. Salvation provides us freedom!

You see, this is how the Helmet of Salvation acts as a piece of protective equipment. When the knowledge of our salvation becomes a constant mental filter, our perspective changes. When we choose that every thought, every attitude, every word, and every action must pass through the barrier of remembering that we are forgiven and delivered from our sins and that we have the hope of eternal life in Heaven, we cannot live as we did before. The purpose of our lives shifts from pleasing ourselves or other people toward focusing on pleasing God.

When the hope of our salvation is continuously at the forefront of our minds, we will be able to stand against any attack of doubt or fear or temptation that the enemy throws at us. When we are tempted or attacked by the enemy, we will be able to answer, *"Because Jesus provided my Salvation, I will not be defeated, but I will choose to 'put on the helmet of salvation' and overcome."*

6. Sword of the Spirit

We need to use the Word of God as a sword to tear down the

devil's evil schemes. Hebrews 4:12 says, *"For the Word of God is alive and active. Sharper than any double-edged sword, it penetrates even to dividing soul and spirit, joints and marrow; it judges the thoughts and attitudes of the heart." (NIV)*

What did Jesus do when the enemy tried to get Him to sin? He fought back using God's Word. (Matthew 4:1-4)

If we want to live as victorious Christians and overcome the attacks of our spiritual enemy, we'll have to do what Jesus did. We need to make Bible reading, study, and memorization a priority in our lives.

If we want to follow Jesus' example and walk in His steps in spiritual warfare, we've got to start by following His example by hiding God's Word in our hearts. Psalm 119:11 says, *"I have hidden your word in my heart that I might not sin against you." (NIV)*

Jesus could use the Word of God as a weapon because Jesus knew what the Word of God said. One of the biggest reasons modern-day Christians aren't living as victorious Christians, but falling prey to the enemy's attacks, is that there is an epidemic of Biblical illiteracy. Too many Christians don't read the Bible, so they don't know what it says. The fundamental truth is that if you aren't reading the Bible and hiding God's Word in your heart, you won't be able to use it as a weapon when the enemy attacks. Instead, when the enemy attacks, you'll go to pull out your spiritual gun and find that you have no ammunition.

Guys, it's time to get dressed! This is where the rubber meets the road.

Will you commit to getting dressed daily to take full advantage of the spiritual wardrobe that God has given to each of us? In order to rise, we have to be dressed and ready to face whatever the day brings us. The enemy WILL take his shot at you, are you dressed and ready to go?

The only question left to ask is, *"What are you waiting for?"*

Today, are you going to choose to *"put on"* the spiritual armor that God has given you, or are you going to be a wimpy, defeated victim that falls into every trap the enemy sets for you?

This is where the rubber meets the road.

Will you put on the Buckle of Truth? Will you choose to live your life in complete and absolute truth, reject the lies of our society, reject the lies about yourself, and live by the absolute truth as defined in the Word of God?

Are you going to wear the Breastplate of Righteousness? Will you, as a Christian, make a conscious decision to choose to abandon sin in your life and live a righteous life every day? Will you choose to do the right thing---the righteous thing---to protect yourself from the enemy's plans to destroy and devour you?

Are you going to put on the Shoes of Peace? As you enter into each new day, will you commit to walking in peace and exhibit self-control, even when it seems like everyone in the world is trying to steal your peace?

Will you carry the Shield of Faith? Will you choose to put on faith daily and believe that God exists, that He is Who He claims to be in the Bible? Do your beliefs about God influence every part of your life until you are a radical follower of Jesus Christ?

Have you decided *"take up"* or *"put on"* the Helmet of Salvation by choosing to give salvation and all that it means control and domination of your mind? Are you training your brain to have every thought, every action, every emotion, and behavior to pass through the filter of *"Because I am justified by Christ, I will think or do...."*?

Are you living your life from an eternal perspective because your mind is wearing the Helmet of Salvation?

Is your #1 weapon the Sword of the Word of God? Are you following Jesus' example and reading, studying, and memorizing God's Word in preparation to use God's Word as a mighty sword to overcome the enemy's attacks?

You see, it's the answers to these questions that tell you, *"Am I really obeying the Bible's command to 'Put on the full armor of God' or am I just pretending to be wearing the armor while I'm really storing it away in my spiritual closet?"*

Get up, Get Dressed, and Get Ready to SHINE!

Group Study Questions:

1. Why is it so important to have spiritual absolutes and truths—things we believe to be true no matter what?

2. What is one area you need to change in your life to walk in holiness and righteousness?

3. What is robbing you of peace in your life? What changes can you make to change this area and gain peace?

4. How does faith protect us from the enemy's attack?

5. How does our salvation guard our minds?

6. Why is the Word of God the primary weapon we have to fight back against attack? Why is it so crucial for us to know God's Word?

7. After reading this chapter, what is one thing you will put into practice or one thing you will change in your life?

8. How can we, as a group, help you do this?

CHAPTER SEVEN
STANDING FIRM

In 2016, one thing divided our country more than anything else in recent memory. It turned family against family, neighbor against neighbor, father against son, friends against friends. It was the question everyone was asking each other on Facebook... **"Who are you backing?"**

No one knew who was going to win, and everyone had an opinion on the topic. You had to pick a side; there was no room for neutrality. We were all forced to be courageous and declare where our loyalties lie. Where you Team Iron Man or Team Captain America?

The movie *"Captain America: Civil War"* was a Hollywood Blockbuster. Because of my love for Tony Stark, I was Team Iron Man. Being honest with you, while this movie was an epic piece of cinema featuring a record number of superheroes, basically the non-official third Avengers Movie, it was probably my least favorite of the Avengers' series. It was definitely my least favorite of the *"Captain*

America Trilogy". It was SO heavy and so serious with very little of the humor or light-hearted moments for which Marvel movies were famous. Take away the Spiderman bits, and it had zippo humor!

However, there is one quote from this movie that really stuck out to me. At Peggy's funeral, they use a famous quote from Christopher Markus:

"Compromise where you can. Where you can't, don't. Even if everyone is telling you that something wrong is something right. Even if the whole world is telling you to move, it is your duty to plant yourself like a tree, look them in the eye, and say 'No, you move'."[1]

The older I get, the more I believe in the importance of having strong personal convictions—unshakeable beliefs that you are willing to fight for, to die for, or, more commonly, to stand firm on.

I say that standing firm happens more often because, at least until now, most Christians in America have not had to take civil action, go to prison, or risk death for their faith as so many who have gone before us. I'm well aware that this may change in the days ahead; however, it isn't a common experience for now. Instead, most believers today are called to *"stand firm"*—to plant themselves like a tree against family, friends, and a society that calls us to be *"tolerant."* Essentially, they want us to *"bend."* They implore us to be *"flexible"* on essential convictions that are immovable.

Among these convictions is the belief that:

• There is only One God, and He created the universe.

• All religions are not equal. The only way to achieve salvation and spend eternity in Heaven is by accepting Jesus as your personal Savior and repenting of your sin.

• Even though grace is free, Christians are called to live in a way that pleases God.

- The belief that the Bible is the infallible Word of God.

- The conviction that the Bible is still relevant and applicable today. We still need to obey what it says.

- The belief that if the Bible calls something *"sin,"* it is *"sin,"* no matter what society says. This includes so many of the prevalent sins that our world now glorifies as normal, socially acceptable, and modern.

As Christians living in the twenty-first century, these convictions are frequently coming under attack. Still, they are areas where we cannot compromise but must, as the quote says, *"Plant ourselves like a tree and say, 'I'm not moving.'"*

Of course, when it comes to the topic of convictions, these are the obvious points. The less obvious and often more difficult situations to face are the real-life circumstances where it would be genuinely easier to compromise our personal beliefs than take a stand. It's the areas where our thoughts tell us, *"It's no big deal—it isn't life or death—just a little compromise will make your life so much easier"* that tends to trip us up.

It's the temptation to stop obeying the Bible and tithing 10% of your income when you're going through financial difficulty.

It agrees to pay someone under the table even though you know it's illegal.

It's choosing to lie just to keep things simpler.

You are compromising your conviction to go along with the crowd or avoid offending someone.

These are the times that cause the rubber to meet the road as we ask ourselves, *"Am I a man who is guided by his convictions, or do I flounder and abandon my convictions when the going gets tough?"*

Throughout my life, I have always believed that I was a man of strong convictions. I've always been passionate about what I believed and done my best to stand by those convictions, no matter what. And yet, it wasn't until I reached my late thirties or early forties that I truly saw the importance of identifying my convictions. By that, I mean taking time to sit down and make a list of beliefs and convictions that I was unwilling to bend on. As always, this decision was the result of hard times—moments when people asked me to *"bend,"* and I realized I just could not.

AM I A MAN WHO IS GUIDED BY HIS CONVICTIONS, OR DO I FLOUNDER AND ABANDON MY CONVICTIONS WHEN THE GOING GETS TOUGH?

In my late thirties and early forties, these options presented themselves over and over again. One of the first times was when we received an invitation to attend a same-sex wedding. It was a few months after my Mom died, and trust me when I say that my Mom would not have received that invite! She was a woman of strong convictions, and everyone knew she wouldn't go.

However, Mom was in Heaven, and people were wondering whether Adessa and I would hold to her convictions or take a more liberal approach. They didn't have to wonder for long. I could not compromise what I believed and attend the ceremony even though I loved the people getting married and prayed for them.

The next big challenge came when our very old car began giving us trouble. The standard advice was, *"Trade it in for a newer one."* The only problem was that we had committed to following *"Dave Ramsey's Money Managing Principles"* and avoiding debt. Not only had we made this commitment, but I was teaching on the topic. Only now it wasn't theoretical—I had to decide to practice what I preached or compromise. We chose to get the car fixed and keep saving money. Years later, God honored our decision and helped us find a fantastic car at an unbelievably low price. Still, that was **after** we chose to stand firm to our convictions.

These challenges were nothing compared to what we would face in the future as Christians, fellow believers, asked us to compromise. Using arguments like *"It's no big deal if you just don't report that money to the IRS"* or *"Why do you have to be so legalistic in your choices of entertainment?"*, time and again, I have been forced to be brave, put on my big boy pants, and say, *"I'm sorry, I can't compromise."*

The hardest one for me was when a friend that I deeply admire and trusted told me to change a message that I truly believed the Holy Spirit asked me to share. For weeks, we went back and forth as this friend tried to convince me I was wrong, and they were right. This was truly heart wrenching for me because I loved my friend and hated having to say *"No"* to them. I spent so much time praying about this situation, but I felt no release to change. Eventually, my friend apologized and admitted that they were wrong, but until we got there, the struggle inside me was real! I didn't like standing up to my friend, and yet, this friend was asking me to go against a personal conviction. I just couldn't do it.

Why? Because deep inside, I knew that if I *"bent"* and compromised my deep conviction, I would be disobeying God and compromising my integrity.

At the end of the day, I'm the one who has to look in the mirror and respect what I see. I'm the one who is going before God in prayer, knowing that I put pleasing someone else over pleasing Him. Ultimately, I'm the one who will have to give account to God for my life. This includes every decision, every word, and every compromise. (Matthew 12:36-37) When that day comes, I want to hear Him say, *"Well done,"* not *"What were you thinking?"*

This is why I believe it is so vital for all of us to be men of conviction. It means taking time to identify what we believe and how far we are willing to go to stand by those beliefs.

One thing that helped me through this process was sitting down and making a list of beliefs that I could not compromise. Obviously, this list included the essential beliefs I listed at the top; however, it also contained personal convictions that I cannot abandon.

It's so important that we don't minimize the value of personal convictions, even if they seem insignificant in the grand scheme of things. Because over the years, I have learned that how we respond when our personal convictions are questioned helps us prepare for the times when our concrete beliefs are attacked.

There's a Scripture in Jeremiah that says,

> *If you have raced with men on foot and they have worn you out, how can you compete with horses? If you stumble in safe country, how will you manage in the thickets by the Jordan? -Jeremiah 12:5, (NIV)*

IDENTIFY WHAT YOU BELIEVE AND HOW FAR YOU ARE WILLING TO GO TO STAND BY THOSE BELIEFS.

In this passage, Jeremiah complained to God about all he suffered because He was God's prophet. Rather than saying, *"Oh, poor Jeremiah,"* God spoke these words, which essentially say, *"Suck it up Buttercup, you ain't seen nothing yet. If you aren't strong enough to stand up to a little suffering, what are you going to do when major persecution comes?"* (My paraphrase, but if you read a commentary, that's the gist.)

Here's how the principle applies to us: Sometimes God allows us to experience a little suffering as we stand up for our personal convictions to teach us how to stand firm in the face of significant persecution regarding the unshakeable truths of God's kingdom.

Every time we stand firm in our convictions, we grow stronger. Our convictions deepen. We are less likely to *"bend"* with every new theory and more likely to stand firm and say, *"No, you move."*

I've seen this happen in my own life. Even though I've always wanted to be a man with deep convictions, it wasn't until my beliefs were tested that I could really claim the title. As is true with so much, it is the difficulties in life that make us shine —be who we genuinely are—and fulfill our purpose in life.

> **EVERY TIME WE STAND FIRM IN OUR CONVICTIONS, WE GROW STRONGER. OUR CONVICTIONS DEEPEN.**

As I look back on my life, I'm thankful for the challenges to my convictions. They made me stronger. They proved to me that God honors our faithfulness to Him and His Word. They helped me understand what it means to plant yourself like a tree and stand firm.

Guys, this book is a call to rise and shine. We have spent the majority of the time so far sharing how to rise. This chapter is KEY to discuss before moving on to Part 2 and looking at how we are to shine. You will only shine if you have the personal convictions inside to know what you believe, and the iron will to stand firm in your beliefs. Only then can you truly shine the truth to a hurting and needing world.

Group Study Questions:

1. Why is it so important for a man of God to have personal convictions that we refuse to back down from?

2. Are you a man who is guided by his convictions, or do you flounder and abandon your convictions when the going gets tough?

3. In this chapter, we stated, *"Sit down and make a list of beliefs that you will not compromise on."* What are some of your convictions that you will not back down from?

4. In this chapter, we stated, *"Every time we stand firm in our convictions, we grow stronger. Our convictions deepen."* Have you found this to be true in your life? How?

5. After reading this chapter, what is one thing you will put into practice or one thing you will change in your life?

6. How can we, as a group, help you do this?

PART TWO:

SHINING

BRIGHT

CHAPTER EIGHT
FEELING DARKNESS

Do you remember field trips in school? I always loved going on a field trip because it meant a day away from classes doing something fun, and usually, it involved lunch at McDonald's. You can't beat that!

Growing up so close to Hershey, Pennsylvania meant a yearly trek to Chocolate World, the virtual tour of a Hershey's Chocolate factory. We did this EVERY year. If you want to know how to make chocolate, I'm your guy!

Of course, this wasn't our only field trip destination. I remember one particular field trip really well. We went on a cave tour where they took us 1,800 feet deep into a coal mine via a small train. One thing I remember was how cold it was in the cave. But something I will never forget is what they did once we were deep inside the cave, away from the opening and sunlight.

The cave was very well lit. Inside, you could see all the

stalagmites and stalactites really well. But once we were deep inside the cave, they wanted us to experience what the cave was like without the lights. They told us to stay in our seats and not move, and they turned off the cave lights.

I had never experienced complete darkness like this before. There was zero light, you couldn't see anything, not even your own hand in front of your face. You could FEEL the darkness. It felt heavy, oppressive, overwhelming, and controlling. You felt like you were completely alone. There was no way to move forward or make progress. You were stuck where you were, unable to move, unable to get your bearings. You had zero control, and you felt hopeless, alone, and afraid. I was thrilled when they finally flipped the light back on! The light consumed the darkness and took with it all those feelings I described.

Looking back on this experience, I think, *"It's no wonder that the Bible refers to a life of sin, separated from God, as darkness."*

The world around us is living in utter darkness. They are trapped in their sins and bondages. They feel the darkness. It leaves them feeling hopeless and alone. They live in oppression and feeling like there is no way out. Many try to hide feeling this way, and some don't realize they feel this way because it is all they have ever know.

In one of my favorite movies, *"The Dark Knight Rises,"* Batman faces off in a battle with Bane. In the scene, Bane is kicking Batman's butt, so Batman uses tech to kill all the lights to make Bane have to fight him in darkness. At this point, Bane says to Batman,

"Oh, you think darkness is your ally. But you merely adopted the dark; I was born in it, moulded by it. I didn't see the light until I was already a man, by then it was nothing to me but BLINDING! The shadows betray you, because they belong to me!" [1]

Bane grew up in the darkness. He knew the night. Even when

experiencing life exposed to light, he still thrived best in darkness. It's what he knew, and it's where he was comfortable.

People who have lived their entire lives in sin and separated from God are used to their darkness. It is all they have ever known. It is where they are comfortable. It is where they thrive. They don't understand how amazing, how freeing life in the light is. Men, it's our job to show them!

OUR ENTIRE PURPOSE IN LIFE IS TO BE A BRIGHT LIGHT IN A DARK WORLD.

It's what Jesus called us to do. He called us to shine bright!

> *You are the light of the world. A town built on a hill cannot be hidden. Neither do people light a lamp and put it under a bowl. Instead they put it on its stand, and it gives light to everyone in the house. In the same way, let your light shine before others, that they may see your good deeds and glorify your Father in heaven*
> *-Matthew 5:14-16 (NIV)*

I love the Message translation of these verses.

> *You're here to be light, bringing out the God-colors in the world. God is not a secret to be kept. We're going public with this, as public as a city on a hill. If I make you light-bearers, you don't think I'm going to hide you under a bucket, do you? I'm putting you on a light stand. Now that I've put you there on a hilltop, on a light stand—shine! Keep open house; be generous with your lives. By opening up to others, you'll prompt people to open up with God, this generous Father in heaven.*

Our entire purpose in life is to be a bright light in a dark world. Our life should be an example to others, something they can strive for, something they dare to dream of obtaining. We are to show the world what it's like to live outside of the darkness.

We are on this earth to shine bright to the world. We have the hope, the peace, the freedom for which they are longing. We have a life free of the oppression of darkness, a liberating life that is wrapped in hope. God calls us to rise so that we can then shine **HIS** light out into a dark world.

We see an excellent picture of this in the Old Testament. In the book of Exodus, we read of the nation of Israel being held captive in the land of Egypt. They were slaves. They were beaten and abused. But then, God decided to set them free. He used Moses (played by Charleton Heston, lol) to go to Pharaoh and negotiate the release of Israel's nation from captivity. However, Pharaoh wasn't really interested in getting rid of his free labor, and he refused to let them go.

God decided to send plagues against the nation of Egypt. One of those plagues was darkness. Let's look at this passage in Exodus:

> *God said to Moses: "Stretch your hand to the skies. Let darkness descend on the land of Egypt—a darkness so dark you can touch it."*

> *Moses stretched out his hand to the skies. Thick darkness descended on the land of Egypt for three days. Nobody could see anybody. For three days no one could so much as move. Except for the Israelites: they had light where they were living. -Exodus 10:21-23 (The MSG)*

The entire nation of Egypt was consumed with utter darkness. It was so dark they could touch it. They couldn't move. They couldn't function. All they could do was sit and endure the darkness.

In their state of darkness, they could see in the distance a glimmer of glow coming from the direction of the Israelites camps.

Stuck in their darkness, the hope of light was there, they just didn't have it. They were trapped in darkness.

As Christians, we are like the nation of Israel. We are the light to those in darkness. We are the flashlight to a person stumbling around during a blackout. We are the headlights for the person driving down a dark country road. We shine bright for them. We have come out of the darkness, and we shine the light the world needs.

Think back on your life before you were saved. While I believe that Christians are called to leave the past behind us and live in hope and joy of God's future for us, we need to look back at our pre-salvation life from time

WE HAVE COME OUT OF THE DARKNESS, AND WE SHINE THE LIGHT THE WORLD NEEDS.

to time to remember exactly what God has done for us. We have to remember what it felt like to live in darkness, complete darkness. We need to remember who it was that first shone some light our way. We need to remember the hope God's light gave us when we felt hopeless, the freedom He gave us when we felt bound, the joy He gave us when we lived in sadness.

Remembering causes us to feel gratitude to God. But even more, it should inspire us to shine on and offer this same hope to all the hurting people around us still trapped in darkness.

The world is full of people still stuck in that life. Millions of people are still:

• Trapped in pornography

• Stuck in a cycle of anger and rage

• Consumed with deceit and lies

• Prisoners to pain and sorrow

• Bound by shame and depression

The list of darkness that people feel and experience goes on and on. They are trapped, stuck, overwhelmed, and unable to move forward. Many are even unaware that they feel this way because it is all they have ever known. That is why we are called to shine bright, so they can see another alternative to their lives.

Our light shows them they can have hope. They can experience peace. They can have joy. We show them what they are missing, and we cause them to want what we have. We bring them into the light of God's Kingdom, and they will never be the same.

So how do we do it? The remainder of this book will highlight areas of the world that desperately need God's light to shine on them, exposing the darkness. The enemy doesn't want people breaking free of his darkness, so he will try and lie about the light. He will call light darkness and good evil. He is the father of lies, after all.

In the remaining chapters, we will highlight areas where the enemy has distorted the truth of our light and how to reclaim them. We will look at:

• How to shine for life.

• How to shine for purity.

• How to shine against darkness and witchcraft.

• How to shine for healing.

We will take an honest look at how the enemy has distorted these areas and how the world, and sometimes the church, have gone along with this distortion. Then we will look at how we can stand as a light in each of these areas and shine the truth on them.

But for now, we need to make a commitment.

Will you commit yourself to be the light that God has called you to be?

Will you shine bright, even when it isn't popular, or goes against cultural norms?

Will you do whatever it takes to be God's flashlight in a dark world used to living in utter darkness? If so, let's continue together.

Group Study Questions:

1. Why is it so important for men of God to show the unsaved trapped in darkness what it is like to live in the light?

2. In this chapter, we spoke about how Egypt was covered in darkness, and only Israel had light. What did you learn from this Bible story?

3. In this chapter, we stated, *"Our light shows them they can have hope. They can experience peace. They can have joy. We show them what they are missing, and we cause them to want what we have."* What does this mean to you?

4. Will you commit yourself to be the light that God has called you to be?

5. Will you shine bright, even when it isn't popular, or goes against cultural norms?

6. Will you do whatever it takes to be God's flashlight in a dark world used to living in utter darkness?

7. After reading this chapter, what is one thing you will put into practice or one thing you will change in your life?

8. How can we, as a group, help you do this?

CHAPTER NINE
SHINING FOR LIFE

"You're doing it again, aren't you? You are so morbid!"

This is what Adessa said to me the other day when she saw me mulling something over in my mind after hearing a song on the radio. She knew from the look on my face exactly what I was doing. I was adding the song to my list of songs to play at my funeral.

I admit I am weird. Except for a non-life-threatening disability, I am a pretty healthy guy. I exercise regularly, I eat healthily (mostly), and I take care of myself. I am in no danger of dying anytime soon, but I love to think about how I would want my funeral to be. According to Adessa, it is morbid that I spend time planning my funeral.

It's not like I spend all of my time thinking about it, but I do plan it more than most people do. I just love to think of ways to make it a great way to preach the Gospel to unsaved friends and family one last time as they are in a mourning, weakened state at the deep sense of loss they feel over losing such an amazing man (lol). Plus, I want it to be a really good show. After all, you only die once! I want people to remember it!

Life and death are heavy topics, I get it. Some people are more okay talking about it than others. I am fine with it, Adessa hates discussing it. I understand both points of view.

Have you noticed that today's society has lost focus on the value of life? That it is being cheapened? That a callousness has developed? Some place more value over one type of life over another. Even the subject of when life was originally created has been distorted. As men of God, we need to shine for life. We need to shine for the truth that all life is important. We need to speak the truth about where life originated. We need to shine bright for life that is oppressed.

In this chapter, I want to focus on three areas that I believe men of God need to be that unbending tree we discussed in our chapter on convictions. We need to shine the light of truth against these lies the world is trying to prop up as truth. We need to shine bright for life. Let's look at the first area.

1. God created life.

The lies of evolution, the big bang, and a host of other untrue theories of where man came from have pervaded our world. Because so many do not want to acknowledge the existence of God, they deny the truth of Creation and makeup lies.

So where did man come from? The Bible makes it very clear.

> *God said, "Let us make mankind in our image, in our likeness, so that they may rule over the fish in the sea and the birds in the sky, over the livestock and all the wild animals, and over all the creatures that move along the*

ground."

So God created mankind in his own image, in the image of God he created them; male and female he created them. - Genesis 1:26-27 (NIV)

The Bible is clear. God created man in his own image. Man wasn't an upgraded form of an ape or a monkey. He wasn't the result of a big bang in the cosmos. Man wasn't an accident! God, the Maker of the Heavens and the earth, created him. Any other version of creation is a lie!

After God created Adam, he saw Adam was lonely. God decided to make a woman for Adam so he would have companionship.

..for Adam no suitable helper was found. So the Lord God caused the man to fall into a deep sleep; and while he was sleeping, he took one of the man's ribs and then closed up the place with flesh. Then the Lord God made a woman from the rib he had taken out of the man, and he brought her to the man. -Genesis 2:20b-22 (NIV)

So there we have it, God created Adam out of the dust of the ground in His image, and He created Eve from Adam's rib. The Bible clearly lays out for you the truth of Creation.

This point is affirmed by the Assemblies of God position paper on the Doctrine of Creation:

"Both Adam and Eve, male and female, are declared to be made in the "image" and "likeness" of God. These carefully delineated creative acts indicate that humans are distinct from animals. God did not form Adam from some previously existing creature (1 Corinthians 15:39). Any evolutionary theory, including theistic evolution/evolutionary Creationism that claims all forms of life arose from common ancestry, is thereby ruled out."[1]

Many may think, *"But Jamie, that isn't what I learned in school."*

That's because the world hates the idea of God creating anything. They hate God and don't want to give Him glory. So they have adopted the false teaching and lies of evolution and are force-feeding it through the education system.

THEY DEVALUE LIFE, THEY DEVALUE THE TRUTH THAT GOD CREATED MAN WITH A SPECIFIC PLAN.

We know that the Word of God, the Bible, is the absolute truth. It contains no lies. It is the Word of God given to man to guide us through life. Right at the beginning of the Bible, in the very first chapter, it tells us how man was created. That is the end of the argument.

As men, we need to stand for truth. We need to declare that God is the Creator, and we are His creation. If you are a father, it is your job to teach your kids the truth of Creation to counter the lies the school systems are pumping into their heads. I recommend you read the entire Assemblies of God Position Paper on Creation. (The link is in the bibliography.) I also recommend reading *"Evidence That Demands A Verdict"* by Josh McDowell. This timeless Apologetics book has information on Creation and Adam as well. Look for other books on Creationism so that you know what you need to know to educate your children and help them learn the truth about creation.

I was privileged to be able to attend a school that believed in the truth of Creation. They presented the argument of Creationism, as well as evolution. They presented scientific facts. There are a LOT of scientific facts and evidence that support Creationism. These scientific facts are ignored by the other side as they present a slanted, untrue version of Creation. However, it is a lie to say that there is no science for Creationism. There is quite a bit. As a parent, you need to learn about it so that you can share it with your children.

This is a matter of science. The evolutionary side tries to say there was no intelligent design, and we came to be by accident. By doing this, they devalue life, they devalue the truth that God created man with a specific plan.

> *I have made them for my glory. It was I who created them. -Isaiah 43:7 (NLT)*

We were made to bring glory to God. We were made in His image. The secularist, humanists, and evolutionists hate God and don't want to bring him ANY glory. So they lie about Creation. They lie about the meaning of life. They devalue life. They devalue the soul of man. This devalues the truth of eternity.

We must stand in the gap and speak the truth. We were created by God to bring Him glory. He created our bodies, He gave us an eternal soul, and we have a responsibility to love, honor, and serve Him. We cannot allow them to devalue human life and birth... which brings us to our second point.

2. We need to stand against abortion and acknowledge that it is murder.

"Wow, Jamie, that is harsh!"

Is it? I don't think it is. The world is full of voices defending this cause or that group. They are standing up for people of every race, sex, and creed...except for babies. The irony is, these infants need people standing up and defending them more than anyone else. Why? Because they can't do it themselves.

THE WORLD IS FULL OF VOICES DEFENDING THIS CAUSE OR THAT GROUP. THEY ARE STANDING UP FOR PEOPLE OF EVERY RACE, SEX, AND CREED... EXCEPT FOR BABIES.

The world health organization predicts that 56 million innocent babies are aborted each year. 56 MILLION! That is WAY more than drunk driving, cancer, Covid-19, AIDS, and so many other forms of fatality. While all of these causes have advocates, who speaks out for these innocent babies?

I honestly can't fathom that people not only don't advocate against killing these babies, but they put time, money, and energy into advocating for the right to murder them. It is sickening.

It's only getting worse. In the past, pro-abortion advocates, especially in politics, advocated for early-term abortion, but were against late-term abortion. Yet, in 2019, several states passed laws not only allowing abortions up to the point of birth, but in some cases, AFTER, the child is born alive! How horrible!

The truth is, modern science has made people aware that abortion is taking life. We know as early as five weeks that the baby has a heartbeat! Five weeks! Most women don't even recognize they are pregnant that soon. Yet, each year millions choose to end a pregnancy.

People know what they are doing is wrong. How do we know this? Because many of the pro-abortion people who want their baby and carry the pregnancy to full term refer to their *"baby"* throughout the pregnancy. They call it *"he"* or *"she,"* not a *"fetus."* They get an ultrasound of their baby, not a fetus. They don't have *"fetus reveal parties"* or *"fetus showers".* It is a baby unless they don't want it, or it is inconvenient; then, it is a fetus. The pro-abortion lobby exposes their lies via their own hypocrisy.

"But Jamie, abortion is a women's health issue; it doesn't involve us guys."

Um, no! Society wants us to believe that this is a women's issue, and men have no right to speak to it. This is a lie! First of all, both male and female babies are being killed. It affects men as much as women.

Abortion isn't a medical issue, and it isn't even a political issue. It is a sin issue. Women say they have the choice with what to do with their bodies—however, the body that is in question is not theirs—it is the body of the life inside of them. The Bible calls us to speak out for justice and help those who cannot help themselves. This is why abortion is not a woman's issue. It is an issue of life.

As men of God, we should be the voice of these innocent babies. We need to be proudly pro-life and stand against the injustice of abortion. We are the only voice they have. They can't fight for themselves. We must fight for them.

We should support the March for Life. We **MUST** support pro-life politicians and reject any politicians who aren't pro-life. I personally will NEVER support or vote for a pro-choice candidate. Financially, we can support pro-life pregnancy centers, which help women through what may be a difficult time in their life.

We must vocalize the truth that abortion is murder. We must do all we can to shine bright for the truth of life and fight for these innocent children. I would encourage you to educate yourself on this topic and read the Assemblies of God Position Paper titled *"Sanctity of Human Life: Abortion and Reproductive Issues"*. We have a link available in our bibliography. [2]

3. Sex Trafficking Is Slavery.

Did you know that there are over 27,000,000 victims of sex trafficking across the world? 27,000,000 innocent women and little girls are being forced into the sex trade to support a 99,000,000 dollar sex industry. That is heartbreaking.

Franklin Graham's ministry, Samaritan's purse, says, *"This modern-day slavery has become a global crisis with an estimated 27 million victims. Some are taken by force. Others are deceived by promises of a better life. By force or coercion, trafficking victims are compelled to work against their will in a wide range of settings, including factories, brothels, houses, streets, farms, and fishing boats. Many are abused beyond comprehension."* 3

It is heartbreaking to think about this, but we can't bury our heads in the sand. As men of God, we need to take a stand for life and against the trafficking of women and children.

As men of God, we need to shine brightly against this horrible form of slavery. It is disgusting how these little girls, teens, and women are being degraded, brutalized, abused, and used, all for money. IT MUST STOP! It is our job as men of God to shine bright against it.

Men, we need to support groups like Samaritan's Purse, who are fighting against sex trafficking and fighting for the victims. Make fighting this issue a focal point of service for your men's ministry by doing fundraisers, etc., to raise support for ministries on the front lines fighting the good fight. Find ways to make a difference.

ONE HUGE WAY TO SHINE FOR LIFE AND STAND AGAINST HUMAN TRAFFICKING IS TO FIGHT AGAINST PORNOGRAPHY.

One huge way to shine for life and stand against human trafficking is to fight against pornography. Think about it. Porn degrades women and devalues them. It makes it seems like they are only good for sexual needs. It doesn't promote female intelligence, success, or any attribute of a woman except her appearance or sexual allure. It degrades women, which degrades life.

Pornography promotes abuse. Covenant Eyes cites: *"A highly cited study from Dr. Gail Dines found that 90% of porn videos contain some combination of degrading physical and verbal aggression, specifically toward women. That content rewires the brain to believe degradation of women is normal."* 4

Every woman in a porn video is somebody's daughter. She is somebody's sister. Would you want other men ogling, fantasizing, degrading, and abusing your mother, daughter, wife, or sister? Of course not! So why is it okay for it to happen to somebody else's mother, daughter, wife, or sister?

Honestly, this is one of the biggest ways men cover or dim their light. They are addicted to porn. Guys, we must break this addiction. We must gain victory. We must shine bright for holiness, purity, and life.

Do whatever you have to do to break free.

Use Covenant Eyes to avoid internet porn. Sign up with the code *Mantour* and get 30 free days!

Find brother's-in-Christ to hold you accountable.

Start seeing women through the eyes of God, not the eyes of an over-sensualized world.

I truly believe these are three HUGE areas that the enemy and society have distorted and lied about the value of life. As men of God, we need to talk about this seriously and shine bright for life in all we say and do.

"But Jamie, I don't want to get involved in politics."

This isn't politics—it's life or death. Too often, these things are looked at as political issues when they are sin issues. These are issues of morality, right and wrong. When we abandoned the truth that God created man in His image, we devalue life. It isn't a political problem. It's a sin problem. As men of God, we are called to stand against sin and for righteousness. We need to stand in the gap. We must shine bright for life!

Group Study Questions:

1. How does evolution devalue life? How does Creationism value life?

2. Why is it so important for a man of God to be opposed to abortion?

3. Why is abortion not a women's health issue, but a life issue?

4. How does sex-trafficking devalue life?

5. What are some actions we, as a group, can take to fight against sex-trafficking?

6. How does pornography devalue life?

7. After reading this chapter, what is one thing you will put into practice or one thing you will change in your life?

8. How can we, as a group, help you do this?

CHAPTER TEN

OLD TIME RELIGION

Recently, I had a chance to do something two nights a week that I hardly ever get to do: watch whatever I want on TV! Adessa was leading a couple of different online Bible studies, leaving me with some alone time. At the time, it was a cold, rainy spring, so there wasn't anything to do outside. I had time to kill, and the remote was all mine. Goodbye Hallmark channel, hello man time!

I rewatched a few of Sylvester Stallone's greatest movies. I revisited some of my favorite superheroes. I even went back and watched some classic NFL games, including one of the happiest nights of my life, when **MY** Denver Broncos won their first Super Bowl (something my friends who are Eagles fans didn't enjoy for another 20+ years!). I even rewatched *"The Drive,"* when John Elway broke Cleveland Browns fans' hearts almost 35 years ago (the Browns never recovered!).

It was so weird rewatching these old games. The technology was SO outdated. We've become accustomed to watching football in 4k, seeing every blade of grass on the field, having amazing replay angles, and having every modern graphic and camera angle. These old games had basically three or four camera angles. The picture was pixelated. There was no first-down yellow line on the field. The graphics looked like they were straight out of Nintendo 64.

Even the game itself was so different. It seemed slower. There were very few big, downfield plays. The NFL style of play was so different from today. This game was so old-fashioned and outdated, from an era gone bye.

I was thinking a lot about this while game-planning for this next chapter. Why? Because one of the biggest lies the enemy is spreading to cause us to dim our lights and not shine brightly is that the Gospel is so outdated.

Think about it. How often do you see on Facebook or Twitter, or hear it on the news, that people who hold to the teaching of the Bible are, at best, old-fashioned prudes, at worst, racist, bigoted, homophobic, and full of hate?

But the truth is that the Bible is God's Word and is still relevant today. This is an area where Christians must rise and shine. The words in the Bible are under attack. People don't believe the Bible is relevant today. They feel it is old-fashioned and has no place in today's open, acceptable society.

THE BIBLE IS GOD'S WORD AND IS STILL RELEVANT TODAY.

I was recently watching a tv show based around the White House. One of the characters was running for President. He was getting hammered in the media because he wouldn't commit to attending a church service. (This was an OLD tv show, today, he'd get hammered if he did go!) He sat down to talk with the current President, and he told him he couldn't go to church because he had given up on God. He read some stuff he didn't like in the Bible, and he walked away from God altogether.

What did the out-going President answer? He said, *"Ah, you can't take the Bible literally."*

Uh, yes, you can. You must! The Bible is the literal word of God. It never changes.

The Bible is still active and relevant today.

> ***All Scripture is God-breathed and is useful for teaching, rebuking, correcting and training in righteousness. - 2 Timothy 3:16 (NIV)***

This verse shows us that the Bible is still of use to us today. It is our guidebook for life. It is God's instructional manual for how to live.

What the Bible says is wrong **REALLY IS WRONG**. If the Bible says to avoid something, **WE MUST AVOID IT.** If the Bible tells us to live a certain way and do certain things, **WE MUST OBEY.** There is no highway option when it comes to God's Word.

The world is trying to discredit the Word of God because it wants to justify its sinful ways. We must stand up for the truth of God's Word and live out what it teaches us.

As men of God, we need to shine brighter than ever! We need to shine for the truth to a world that loves living in lies. I want to look specifically at a few areas we need to shine for truth, areas the world says the Bible is wrong about.

1. Sex is for a husband and wife only.

The Bible is very clear when it comes to the topic of sex and marriage, and it is different than today's cultural norms. The Bible is clear; sex is for the marriage bed between a husband and wife. This is how God ordained sex to be. **NOTHING** else is permitted under God's Word.

Quite the contrary. The Bible is explicit and clear. Homosexuality is a sin. Living together before marriage is a sin. We are not to have sex before we get married. We are not to sleep with anyone other than our spouse after marriage. It really is simple. You meet a girl, get married, and then have sex...in that order. Any other order or arrangement is a sin before God and must be repented off.

> *But 'God made them male and female' from the beginning of creation. 'This explains why a man leaves his father and mother and is joined to his wife, and the two are united into one.' Since they are no longer two but one, let no one split apart what God has joined together.*
> *-Mark 10:6-9 (NLT)*

> *God's will is for you to be holy, so stay away from all sexual sin. Then each of you will control his own body and live in holiness and honor— not in lustful passion like the pagans who do not know God and his ways. Never harm or cheat a fellow believer in this matter by violating his wife, for the Lord avenges all such sins, as we have solemnly warned you before. God has called us to live holy lives, not impure lives. Therefore, anyone who refuses to live by these rules is not disobeying human teaching but is rejecting God, who gives his Holy Spirit to you.*
> *-1 Thessalonians 4:3-8 (NLT)*

> *Don't you realize that those who do wrong will not inherit the Kingdom of God? Don't fool yourselves. Those who indulge in sexual sin, or who worship idols, or commit adultery, or are male prostitutes, or practice homosexuality, or are thieves, or greedy people, or drunkards, or are abusive, or cheat people—none of these*

will inherit the Kingdom of God.
-1 Corinthians 6:9-10 (NLT)

The good news is, there is forgiveness for this sin. If you have had sex before marriage, if you have engaged in homosexual practices, if you have been unfaithful, God will forgive you. There will still be consequences for these actions, but forgiveness is yours if you repent and turn away from your sin and stop.

I know of people who had been living together before they were saved. After accepting Christ, they realized that they were sinning against God, so they moved out and got their own place until their wedding. I know of people living a homosexual lifestyle, but they came to Christ, became Christians, and left this lifestyle behind because they discovered it was a sin.

I have known men who were sexually active outside of marriage, but when they came to Christ, they realized it was sin, and committed themselves to a life of celibacy until they got married. They couldn't get their virginity back obviously, but they committed to no more sex from this point until their wedding.

All of these are examples of people who repented of their sin and changed their lifestyle to conform to God's Word. However, one problem is that in today's church, too many people call themselves *"Christians,"* repent of their sin, but do not change their lifestyle to stop sinning. Why? Because they will not accept the truth that the Bible is still relevant today.

WE NEED TO STAND FIRM AND SHINE BRIGHT TO A DARK WORLD THE TRUTH OF SEX FOR A MAN OF GOD.

Instead, they believe the lie of progressive Christianity that the Bible is no longer applicable in today's society. However, this isn't true. While forgiveness is available, and we are offered every chance to start again, being a Christian still means that we obey God's Word and stop sinning, even if that means changing our lifestyle.

No matter what the world says or what attacks they lay at our feet, God's Word is clear when it comes to the place for sex. When it comes to the truths of sex for a man of God, we need to stand firm and shine bright in a dark world.

2. There is only one true God.

One of the biggest lies the enemy is using today is that it is okay to worship any god; we need to be inclusive of all people and religions. The world is continually labeling the church as bigoted and hateful when we reject false religions and false gods. But the Bible is VERY clear. There is only one true God.

> *For there is one God, and one mediator between God and men, the man Christ Jesus. -1 Timothy 2:5 (NIV)*

> *One God and Father of all, who is above all, and through all, and in you all. - Ephesians 4:6 (NIV)*

> *As concerning therefore the eating of those things that are offered in sacrifice unto idols, we know that an idol is nothing in the world, and that there is none other God but one. For though there be that are called gods, whether in Heaven or in earth, (as there be gods many, and lords many,) But to us there is but one God, the Father, of whom all things, and we in him; and one Lord Jesus Christ, by whom are all things, and we by him. -1 Corinthians 8:4-6 (KJV)*

> *And this is life eternal, that they might know thee the only true God, and Jesus Christ, whom thou hast sent. -John 17:3 (KJV)*

As believers, we cannot go along with the lie that all religions are good and equal. To do so is condemning people to a life in Hell.

Jesus is the one way to Heaven (John 14:6). We are not hateful or bigoted when we say this; we are actually loving. It kills me to think about people devoting their lives to worshiping a god who cannot save them from their sins. It makes me so sad to think about how devastated a devout follower of another religion must be when they die and face their judgment. They were deceived, but they truly believed it and followed the teaching to a "*t*", only to find it was for naught because it was a false religion. That is so sad, so heartbreaking.

We cannot go along with this teaching that all roads, all religions, lead to Heaven. It simply isn't true. It isn't loving or kind to do this. The truth is there is only one way, and it is Jesus.

3. There is a supernatural world, and we need to take it seriously.

I want to look at this point from two different perspectives: how the world sees the supernatural world, and how the church sees it. Let's start with the church.

I have found that in today's modern church, the Christian community steers a wide path around the topic of the supernatural. Too often, they fear it will make them look creepy or weird to the world. They don't want to touch the subject of angels or demons, demonic activity, and possession, or any other area of the supernatural that they think is *"too freaky."*

Not only that, but many are willing to not only ignore it, but actually to embrace it. Twenty years ago, in the church, you never would have had believers watching magic, yet today believers don't change the channel when the magicians perform on America's Got Talent. Some churches even invite magicians to perform at their outreaches! In the past, witches, wizards, and warlocks would have been shunned by Christians who didn't want it influencing them spiritually. Now we line up to see *"Doctor Strange"* or read or watch the latest *"Harry Potter"* books and movies. AND we open them up to our children!

WHAT ARE WE DOING? News flash.... there is a spiritual, dark world. It is run by Satan, and he is using it to trap too many believers into darkness. We are opening ourselves up to the demonic world like never before, and it is making the church today sick and weak, all in the name of entertainment.

Sometimes I think the world takes the supernatural more seriously than the church. They certainly don't walk around acting like it doesn't exist. The world gets it. TV shows, movies, and podcasts are devoted to the topic of the supernatural, ghosts, demons, etc. How often do you hear the unsaved refer to someone struggling as *"wrestling with their demons"*? The world knows there is a supernatural realm. Yet the church runs from such concepts so that we don't weird people out.

HERE IS A SPIRITUAL, DARK WORLD. IT IS RUN BY SATAN, AND HE IS USING IT TO TRAP TOO MANY BELIEVERS INTO DARKNESS.

People get attacked by demons. Jesus was continually setting people free of demonic oppression and possession. Why don't we as believers want to see people receive this same freedom? Why don't we give them the hope of a peaceful, pure heart and mind, free of demonic oppression?

The enemy uses yoga, ouija boards, magic, science fiction, comic books, literature, entertainment, and the list goes on and on, to spread darkness and oppression. As men of God, we must realize that we must stand against this evil. We must shine the light of truth against this dark kingdom. We must fight back against demonic attacks. We need to help the possessed and oppressed find freedom and victory. It is not old-fashioned; it is active and present in today's day and age.

I am sure this entire chapter has shocked a few of you with how tough it was. Truth like I have written is not talked about much today because society has been winning this particular battle by convincing the world, and unfortunately, many in the church, that we need to be more tolerant and loving. But the truth is that love is dripping from every word I have written. It is cruel to allow people to continue in sin or to follow a path that leads to false religion or demonic oppression. Love shines the light of truth and helps them find what we all need now more than ever: freedom, hope, peace, and salvation.

SPIRITUAL WARFARE IS NOT OLD-FASHIONED; IT IS ACTIVE AND PRESENT IN TODAY'S DAY AND AGE.

This is the main problem with modern progressive Christianity: It sounds good when it talks about love and acceptance, but because it is a lie, it leads people to Hell. It is the broad road that Jesus talks about in Matthew 7:13-14. Yet, Jesus warns us not to take that road, but instead, cling to the straight and narrow.

Following Jesus is not like eating at Burger King. You can't have it *"your way right away."* Instead, being a Christian means following Jesus. Following Jesus requires us to accept that every part of the Bible is still relevant today. It lays out the only path to Heaven. We are required to obey it's teaching.

Jeremiah 6:16 says, ***"This is what the Lord says: 'Stand at the crossroads and look; ask for the ancient paths, ask where the good way is, and walk in it, and you will find rest for your souls.' But you said, 'We will not walk in it.'"*** *(NIV)*

Today, we stand at this same crossroads. We have what the world needs. The question is, are you strong enough to shine bright against today's culture? Will you accept that the Bible is still relevant today? Will you commit to living your life by Biblical principles? Will you be a light that speaks truth to a dark world?

Standing at the same crossroads as Jeremiah, will you choose to say, *"This isn't the road I want"* or *"I will wholeheartedly follow Jesus no matter what"?*

The choice lies with each of us. Will we rise? Will we shine? The question is, *"Are you strong enough to shine bright against today's culture and progressive Christianity?"*

Group Study Questions:

1. In this chapter, we stated, *"The words in the Bible are under attack. People don't believe the Bible is relevant today. They feel it is old-fashioned and has no place in today's open, acceptable society."* How have you seen this demonstrated in your sphere of influence?

2. How do we lovingly stand for the Biblical truth that sex is only between a husband and wife?

3. How is Progressive Christianity perverting the truth about sex? How do we combat this?

4. Why is it important to stand for the truth that there is only one true God?

5. What practical changes do you need to make to protect your family from the dangers of the evil, occultic world that is so popular in our society?

6. Are you strong enough to shine bright against today's culture?

7. After reading this chapter, what is one thing you will put into practice or one thing you will change in your life?

8. How can we, as a group, help you do this?

CHAPTER ELEVEN
SHINE A LIGHT ON HEALING

My sister Adessa loves the movie, *"Castaway"*.[1] If you have never seen it, it is about a FedEx efficiency expert played by Tom Hanks whose plane crashes, leaving him alone on a deserted island. The movie shows how he survived for years on the island, and, spoiler alert, how he gets off the island. While on the island, he uses the contents of the FedEx packages that washed up on shore to survive. He uses all the packages except one. The movie ends with him leaving this one unopened package on the doorstep of its destination, years after it was sent.

Shortly after this hit movie debuted, FedEx made a Super Bowl commercial spoofing the ending of the movie. They show the castaway walking up to the house and handing the woman the beaten and battered packaged. Before he leaves, he says, *"By the way, what was in the package?"*

As the woman opened it, she says, *"Oh, nothing much. Just a satellite phone, a GPS locator, a fishing rod, a water purifier, and some seeds. Just silly stuff."*

It was a brilliant, funny commercial. Everything he needed for survival and rescue was in the package that he carried around with him and never opened.

While it is a great commercial, the idea of having everything you need available and never using it is kinda depressing. Yet, every day, believers do this. We have everything a lost and dying world needs, yet we are keeping it to ourselves instead of shining bright and giving it to a lost and hurting world.

In this chapter, I want to look at one HUGE blessing and gift that God has given to His children that, unfortunately, too many believers hide away. We dim the light over this particular blessing because we don't want to be embarrassed or ridiculed. But today more than ever, we need to raise that dimmer switch and shine it bright to a hurting and dying world. What is this thing? Healing.

> **WE HAVE EVERYTHING A LOST AND DYING WORLD NEEDS, YET WE ARE KEEPING IT TO OURSELVES INSTEAD OF SHINING BRIGHT AND GIVING IT TO A LOST AND HURTING WORLD.**

I, for the life of me, don't understand why so many believers shy away from the topic of healing. Divine healing is such a fabulous gift our Savior gives to us. Yet few talk about it. Rarely do you hear a sermon on it in today's church. It is just out there, don't look, don't touch.

I have seen first hand how this topic is sorta off-limits for believers. As anyone who has ever seen me in person knows, I suffer from a physical disability that hinders me greatly and causes me great pain. Often when people ask me about my disability, they ask the question, *"Is there anything the doctors can do for you?"* My answer is always the same. I say, *"Not really, it is so far gone, they say there is a surgery they could try, but they can't guarantee it will work, and it requires me to be flat in bed for 12-18 months. I don't have time for that, and even if it helps, it will devolve back to how it is now since it is neurological. My only hope is a healing from God."*

Almost every time I say this, the person's face drops, they look sad, and move on to another topic. They take what I said as a hopeless situation. Rarely do they ask to pray for my healing or encourage me that God has the power to heal. Instead, they accept that I am doomed to a life of pain and disability.

But that in no way is what I mean when I say my only hope is a healing from God. What a tremendous source of hope! I hold onto this and look forward to it. I don't say it sadly or in a defeated attitude, I say it expectingly. Why? Because I serve a God Who heals!

One of Jesus' chief miracles He did on earth was healing people.

Jesus went throughout Galilee, teaching in their synagogues, proclaiming the good news of the kingdom, and healing every disease and sickness among the people. News about him spread all over Syria, and people brought to him all who were ill with various diseases, those suffering severe pain, the demon-possessed, those having seizures, and the paralyzed; and he healed them. -Matthew 4:23-24 (NIV)

The healings didn't just end with Jesus, throughout the book of Acts, we see healings and miracles as people find relief and wholeness through the healing power of God.

Physical healing is still available to us today. Jesus' death and resurrection didn't bring an end to healing. It increased the healing power.

But he was pierced for our transgressions, he was crushed for our iniquities; the punishment that brought us peace was on him, and by his wounds we are healed. -Isaiah 53:5 (NIV)

And the prayer offered in faith will make the sick person well; the Lord will raise them up. If they have sinned, they will be forgiven. -James 5:15 (NIV)

"He himself bore our sins" in his body on the cross, so that we might die to sins and live for righteousness; "by his wounds you have been healed." -1 Peter 2:24 (NIV)

The Assemblies of God website has a quote by our General Superintendant Doug Clay that is so right on when it comes to healing. He said, *"Christ's death on the cross not only provides for forgiveness of sin, but also healing for sickness. The One who gave you the gift of eternal life…is the same One who can heal your body."* 2

Personally, I have experienced divine healing from God. When I was about twelve years old, I had a lump in my wrist that the doctors thought was cancer. I saw the lump on an MRI, and I felt the pain of it. I went forward for prayer that Sunday, and Monday, the lump was gone!

When I was twenty and a sophomore at the University of Valley Forge, I woke up one Sunday morning sick as a dog. I had the worse headache I have ever had. I had a fever, and let's just say that me and the toilet were inseparable. The next day I got worse, and the following day my parents came to get me and take me to the doctor.

The doctor had no idea what was wrong with me, but I kept getting worse. That night my fever rose even higher, and my mom called an ambulance. I remember very little of this 50-minute ambulance ride, and the next few days are fuzzy to me. I know I was hemorrhaging, I couldn't stop going to the bathroom, and my fever spiked to 106-107. I was moved to ICU and packed in ice.

The doctors couldn't figure out what was wrong with me, and

they didn't expect me to live. A pivotal day was the day before my twentieth birthday. My mom, unable to stand the thought of having to go and watch her son die, cried out to God for help. She said at that moment, God told her to make my bed because I was coming home. God's assuring words gave her the strength to face the upcoming day. This was strength which she would truly need.

That same morning my condition got worse. My white blood cell count was dangerously low and falling, causing my body to not be able to fight any germs. I was packed in a bed of ice in an effort to lower my temperature. Later, I learned that the doctors feared that the prolonged high fever would leave me brain dead or paralyzed.

The next day was my birthday, and it turned out to be the most dramatic day of my life. My parents arrived at the hospital to the news that more tests needed to be taken. However, the tests were extremely dangerous. They needed to drain the fluid from my lungs so that I wouldn't drown and die. The doctors where unsure if I would survive this procedure.

I survived the test and spent the rest of my birthday sleeping off the nerve pills they gave me to get me through the tests. The doctors were treating me with the newest, most high powered drugs they could give me, but nothing was working. Later that night, I awoke to a nurse taking my temperature. It was 106 degrees, and the room turned to panic. The nurse immediately packed me in more ice. My white blood cell count was dangerously low and falling, leaving me unable to fight off the infection. I was basically dying.

It was at this point that I mustered the strength to pray the only prayer that I was capable of praying. I said, *"Daddy, please help me. I can't do this myself"*.

At that moment, I heard the voice of God in a way that I had never heard before. He said to me, *"Don't worry. You will be okay. I will take care of you"*.

I felt such a sense of peace come over my entire body. I had no idea it was the power of God. I fell asleep and had the most peaceful night I had experienced since this nightmare began.

The next day I awoke to find that my temperature had dropped to 98.6 degrees, never to rise again. I was given food to eat. It was the first time I had eaten in the past nine days. I laughed and talked to my family. At one point, I laughed so hard that I threw up. My mom later told me that once she saw me laughing, she knew I was all better. Even the doctors said it was a miracle.

The next day I was moved from intensive care into a private room until my white blood cells were established at a safe number. I began physical therapy. I was so weak and had lost 35 pounds in nine days. I had to regain my strength to be able to walk. By the end of the week, I was back at home in my bed. God's words to my mom were fulfilled. It was a miracle.

The healing was a complete miracle from God. No brain damage occurred from prolonged high fever. As a matter of fact, my professors allowed me to take my final exams just a few weeks later from my home. I remembered everything I had learned and passed all the exams with flying colors, including my language class in ancient Biblical Hebrew. My body was completely healed by God. On top of all this, God even went the extra mile and healed my left foot. I now have a perfectly normal foot.

I know from first-hand experience that God has the power to heal. The fact that I have the mental ability to write this chapter is proof of His healing power. It is how I get up every day with the hope that, one day, God will finish the healing and heal my right foot, allowing me to walk pain-free, walk on sand, use an exercise bike or elliptical machine, and a host of other things I hope to do one day after I am healed.

"But Jamie, doesn't it make you mad that God doesn't heal you now?"

Honestly, no. Why? Because I believe everything in my life is being used by God to further His kingdom. If His kingdom can grow more effectively if I am healed, I will be healed. If I can help grow the kingdom more with my disability, than I happily suffer through it if it advances His kingdom.

Honestly, I think the fear of someone not being healed when we pray for them is why so many believers are dimming the switch on healing. They don't want to be embarrassed if they pray, and nothing happens. But isn't that thinking a little arrogant? It puts the power of healing on us, not God. We are the vessel God uses, but HE is the One Who heals.

What do we have to lose when we offer to pray for someone suffering physically? The worst-case scenario is they aren't healed. But what if they are? What if someone's healing is delayed because you won't pray for them? What if their suffering is prolonged because of your fears?

> **WE ARE THE VESSEL GOD USES, BUT HE IS THE ONE WHO HEALS.**

I believe we serve a God Who heals. He heals us physically, but it isn't the only way God heals us.

1. God heals emotions

I believe that God has the power to heal our emotions. He can heal our emotional pain and the trauma we have experienced. Psalms 147:3 says:

He (God) heals the brokenhearted, and binds up their wounds. (NIV)

Revelations 21:4 says: *He (God) will wipe every tear from their eyes. (NIV)*

Psalms 23 tells us God restores our souls. God heals our emotions. He helps us work through the pain and sorrow we have. He is there to help us in our darkest times, and He will gives us everything we need emotionally.

2. God heals minds.

Like it or not, our minds get corrupted and perverted through sin and having a sinful nature. Often times, we allow our minds to be affected and damaged through sin, compromise, and not following God's Word. However, our minds don't have to stay broken and damaged. We serve a God Who heals our minds.

> *Those who live according to the flesh have their minds set on what the flesh desires; but those who live in accordance with the Spirit have their minds set on what the Spirit desires. The mind governed by the flesh is death, but the mind governed by the Spirit is life and peace.*
> *-Romans 8:5-6 (NIV)*
>
> *Do not be conformed to this world, but be transformed by the renewing of your mind. -Romans 12:2 (NASB)*
>
> *Therefore we do not lose heart, but though our outer man is decaying, yet our inner man is being renewed day by day.*
> *– 2 Corinthians 4:16 (NASB)*

The Word of God renews our mind and brings us healing. Spending time in prayer with God helps us focus our thoughts on Him. The power of the Holy Spirit can change our way of thinking.

I know in my life, I used to be a very negative, depressed, moody guy. I looked at everything as a pessimist and with a glass half empty point of view. When I allowed the Holy Spirit to work on me and my issues, He changed my outlook. I am now a happy, optimistic guy. God healed my mind.

3. God heals relationships.

The final area of healing I want to look at is relationships. I truly believe that God can heal relationships when both people are willing to make changes and do things God's way. God will show us areas where we are wrong and the areas we need to change, and if we allow Him, He will change us and restore our relationships.

Growing up, my dad was abusive to me. He kept the abuse a secret by telling me lies about my mom to keep me from telling her about the abuse. This greatly damaged my relationship with my mom. Over the course of years, our relationship became very broken.

However, God healed our relationship. Through counseling and both of us deciding to respond Biblically to our hurts, we came to a place where our relationship was healed. Mom and I had about 7-8 years of a healthy, functional relationship. After she died, I am so grateful for this healing power and the restored relationship.

WE CANNOT KEEP USING A DIMMER SWITCH WHEN IT COMES TO HEALING. TOO MANY PEOPLE NEED GOD'S PHYSICAL TOUCH.

I know firsthand that we serve a healing God. We **CANNOT** keep using a dimmer switch when it comes to healing. Too many people need God's physical touch. People's hearts are aching for God to heal their emotional wounds. Minds need to be renewed and restored through the power of God. Relationships need to be made whole, and reunions need to take place as God heals and restores relationships.

Like the FedEx commercial package had everything the castaway needed to get help, we have what the world needs to be helped, healthy, and whole in body, mind, soul, and spirit. Today, will you commit to letting it shine?

Group Study Questions:

1. Why is it so vital for us to shine bright for healing?

2. What keeps you from asking someone to pray for them when they share a physical issue? What's the worst that could happen?

3. Have you ever experienced a physical healing? Share the story with the group.

4. In this chapter, we stated, *"God heals emotions."* Why is this important? Have you experienced this healing?

5. Why is it so important to allow God to heal our minds?

6. Do you have a relationship that needs to be healed? What can you do to start the healing process?

7. After reading this chapter, what is one thing you will put into practice or one thing you will change in your life?

8. How can we, as a group, help you do this?

CONCLUSION

For the past few days, I have been asking God what the final challenge was He wanted me to bring to you in this book. I have struggled with how to end our time together and what final thought to leave you. As I write this, it is 5 a.m. It is the weekend, the one day I can sleep in and get some much-needed rest. My aging bladder woke me up, but after a quick trip to the bathroom, I could not go back to sleep because this final chapter is now burning in my heart.

It's ironic. This book is about waking up the sleeping giant and standing for what we believe. Of course, God would end the book by asking me to wake up early when I don't want to be awake and write the words He wants you and me to hear. I could have rolled over and gone back to sleep, ignoring the Holy Spirit's prompting, but what if I reawaken later, and the words were not there burning inside of me anymore? I realized I was burning daylight. I had to *rise and shine*, finish this chapter, and share what God has placed on my heart.

So far in this book, we have discussed the need to rise, to no longer stay in our spiritual bed, allowing complacency to dominate our lives. We have discussed that we need to rise and shine because there is a world around us dying and going to hell while we stay asleep. We have examined areas we need to shine bright as the enemy and the world tries to lull everyone into ignoring the truth of God's Word.

I have laid out the case for you to rise and shine. Now we have reached the moment of truth, the moment of decision, the moment we choose once and for all, will we stay in the comfort of our spiritual beds, or will we rise and shine?

I know the emotional response inside of us all is to yell out, *"I will rise! I will shine bright to the world!"*. But emotional responses are just that, emotions. We need to go beyond emotions and make an informed decision.

WILL WE STAY IN THE COMFORT OF OUR SPIRITUAL BEDS, OR WILL WE RISE AND SHINE?

We are where the nation of Israel found themselves centuries ago. God had delivered them from the bondage of Israel. He led them through the desert into the Promised Land. Under Joshua's leadership, they gained victory over the nations around them and secured their land. Freedom, victory, and everything God had promised them, was in their grasp. Joshua knew this, but he also knew the people, and he knew they needed a challenge. They needed to be pushed, so He gave them a challenge that still rings true.

I handed you a land for which you did not work, towns you did not build. And here you are now living in them and eating from vineyards and olive groves you did not plant. So now: Fear GOD. Worship him in total commitment. Get rid of the gods your ancestors worshiped on the far side of The River (the Euphrates) and in Egypt. You, worship GOD.

If you decide that it's a bad thing to worship GOD, then choose a god you'd rather serve—and do it today. Choose one of the gods your ancestors worshiped from the country beyond The River, or one of the gods of the Amorites, on whose land you're now living. As for me and my family, we'll worship GOD." -Joshua 24:13-15 (MSG)

What a rallying cry from Joshua! It equals any speech by William Wallace or John Wayne. He issues this strong rally cry to the nation of Israel, and, in the emotion of the moment, they replied to Joshua.

GOD is our God! He brought up our ancestors from Egypt and from slave conditions. He did all those great signs while we watched. He has kept his eye on us all along the roads we've traveled and among the nations we've passed through. Just for us he drove out all the nations, Amorites and all, who lived in the land.

Count us in: We too are going to worship GOD. He's our God. -Joshua 24:16-18 (MSG)

Joshua knew they were answering out of emotions. He knew they hadn't given it the thought it needed. He knew it was a shallow decision, so he challenged them once again.

Then Joshua told the people: 'You can't do it; you're not able to worship GOD. He is a holy God. He is a jealous God. He won't put up with your fooling around and sinning. When you leave GOD and take up the worship of foreign gods, he'll turn right around and come down on you hard. He'll put an end to you—and after all the good he has done for you!' -Joshua 24:19-20 (MSG)

Not exactly a vote of confidence from Joshua. What a downer statement. But was it? Or is Joshua lovingly making them truly consider the decision they made? I believe he is trying to get them to truly make a firm commitment from the right frame of mind so that they know what they are saying, and even more importantly, they follow through and actually do it. How did the people reply?

> *But the people told Joshua: 'No! No! We worship GOD!'*
>
> *And so Joshua addressed the people: 'You are witnesses against yourselves that you have chosen GOD for yourselves —to worship him.'*
>
> *And they said, 'We are witnesses.'*
>
> *Joshua said, 'Now get rid of all the foreign gods you have with you. Say an unqualified Yes to GOD, the God of Israel.'*
>
> *The people answered Joshua, 'We will worship GOD. What he says, we'll do.'- Joshua 24:21-24 (MSG)*

The decision has been made. Joshua showed them what they had to do to keep the resolution, and they committed to doing it and following through with their decision.

I love this passage of Scripture, especially how Joshua handled it. When was the last time your pastor preached a sermon, issued a challenge at an altar call, and, when you came forward, told you he didn't think you could keep the commitment you are making? I have personally never experienced it! But Joshua wanted them to make an informed decision before they committed to following through.

Joshua was in no way trying to discourage the people. He wasn't trying to get them not to do the right thing. He was simply making sure they knew exactly what they were agreeing to do.

I want to end this book by doing the same thing. I have laid out a path that I believe God is calling His men to in this day and age. It's a path to shine bright to a dark world, a journey to be different, stand for the truth of the Bible, and not waver. I believe it is the only path for a man of God, and I hope you have caught the message of this book and genuinely decide to rise and shine. But do you know what the cost of this may be?

When you rise and shine for God, His ways, and His principles, many people are not going to like you. To honestly do it, you will need to stand against the culture of the world. You will have to stand against people telling you that you are a racist, a homophobe, or a radical extremist. You won't be able to take part in the virtue signaling on social media for causes that are not in line with God's Word. You could have people lie about you. It will not be easy.

You will even have fellow believers do this to you. The Christian community is being infiltrated with a false doctrine right now called Progressive Christianity. This branch of Christianity doesn't believe the Bible is relevant for today. They feel sex in any form is acceptable.

WE NEED TO PUSH ASIDE COMPLACENCY, PUT ASIDE THE NEED FOR APPROVAL FROM OTHERS, AND DECIDE THE ONLY APPROVAL WE NEED IS GOD'S APPROVAL.

Drinking is okay. Social justice is more important to them than the principles of the Bible. They support every cause that rises in society, putting virtue-signaling ahead of obeying God's Word. They corrupt the Word of God to promote sins and the world's culture, all so they can say they are Christians, but not offend anyone. They make it doubly hard for us to rise and shine because they promote to the world that you can be a Christian without actually standing for anything. It is infiltrating the church. It is dangerous. It is rooted in lies from the enemy.

To rise and shine, we need to know what we will have to fight to shine bright. We must resolve in our hearts that pleasing God is more important than pleasing society, and even pleasing progressive and liberal Christians. We have to be willing to shove it aside. We need to push aside complacency, put aside the need for approval from others, and decide the only approval we need is God's approval.

It is not always easy to shine bright, but it is always right. It won't always be popular, but it will be proper. The world and progressive Christians may ridicule you or attack you. But one day, you will stand before God, and He will say, ***"Well done, good and faithful servant...enter into your reward." (Matthew 25:21)***

Personally, I will endure ridicule, harsh words, and mocking from the world to hear these words from God one day. I have made my decision. I am going to rise and shine.

Now is the moment for you to decide. What are you going to do?

- Are you going to throw off those sheets of comfort and complacency and get out of bed?

- Are you going to stay standing and not allow mistakes or sins you may commit to drive you back to the comfort of the covers?

- Are you going to daily wear the wardrobe of a man of God that we discussed in chapters five and six?

- Will you choose to shine bright for God and His ways?

- Will you develop your own convictions based on God's Word and shine brightly for these convictions?

- Will you shine for life and embrace the fight in all its forms?

- Will you shine for truth even when the world tries to convince you that their lies are truth and the Bible's truths are lies?

- Will you shine for the healing power of God to heal bodies, minds, souls, and spirits?

• Do you have what it takes to rise and shine?

It is a decision all men must face and make at some point in life. It is the difference between right and wrong, life and death.

You must make a decision. But let me tell you this. **I believe in you.** I believe that you have what it takes. I believe that you have the strength and power to kick back the covers, rise, to shove complacency, fear, and any other thing keeping you stuck under the covers. I believe you have what it takes to rise and shine, to be the beacon of God's light to a lost and dying world.

What will you choose?

My hope is you choose to rise and shine. **Stop burning daylight!** Answer God's challenge and rise and shine brightly!

Group Study Questions:

1. Are you going to throw off the sheets of comfort and complacency and get out of bed?

2. Are you going to stay standing and not allow mistakes or sins you may commit to drive you back to the comfort of the covers?

3. Are you going to daily wear the wardrobe of a man of God that we discussed in chapters five and six?

4. Will you choose to shine bright for God and His ways?

5. Will you develop your own convictions based on God's Word and shine brightly for these convictions?

6. Will you shine for life and embrace the fight in all its forms?

7. Will you shine for truth even when the world tries to convince you that their lies are truth and the Bible's truths are lies?

8. Will you shine for God's healing power to heal bodies, minds, souls, and spirits?

9. Do you have what it takes to rise and shine?

10. After reading this chapter, what is one thing you will put into practice or one thing you will change in your life?

11. How can we, as a group, help you do this?

BURNING DAYLIGHT

THE GODLY MAN'S CALL TO RISE AND SHINE.

WORKBOOK

Chapter One:

-We have to stop _____ our _____. It's time we, as believers, rise and shine!

-Write down three ways you can do a better job shining God's Light to the world:

1.

2.

3.

Group Study Questions:

1. Why is it important to Rise and Shine?

2. Is there any area of your life where you are using a spiritual dimmer switch?

3. What is your greatest fear of shining bright in a dark world?

4. Is this fear rational? Or would it not be as bad as you think?

5. After reading this chapter, what is one thing you will put into practice or one thing you will change in your life?

6. How can we, as a group, help you do this?

Chapter 2:

-We must take Jesus' words _____ and put them in _____!

-No one could ever _____ _____ to get to Heaven. That is why the only way to Heaven is through _____ in _____.

It is time we rise and shine and fulfill the Great Commission.

We discussed the need to share your personal story with the lost. Take a minute and write down your story:

_____

_____

_____

_____

_____

_____

_____

_____

_____

_____

_____

_____

_____

_____

_____

_____

_____

_____

_____

Group Study Questions:

1. Why do you think Jesus chose to make the Great Commission His final thoughts to His followers?

2. Why is it so essential for us to fulfill the Great Commission?

3. In this chapter, we stated, *"There is a Hell, and good people go there."* What did you think about this point?

4. In this chapter, we stated, *"There is a Heaven, and bad people are there."* What did you think about this point?

5. This chapter talked about sharing your faith by sharing your story. Practice this by sharing your story with the group.

6. After reading this chapter, what is one thing you will put into practice or one thing you will change in your life?

7. How can we, as a group, help you do this?

Chapter Three

-Have you been hitting the spiritual _____
_____?

-If we truly understood the _____ and why it is so
important, a lot less _____, _____,
and snooze alarm hitting would occur.

Write down what your "someday" issue is that you have been delaying
doing for God.

Write three actions you can take to begin doing what God called you
to do:

1.

2.

3.

Group Study Questions:

1. Have you been using the *"someday"* excuse? What is your *"someday"* that you have been putting off?

2. Are you walking in complete obedience to God?

3. Have you delayed doing anything God has asked you to do?

4. Have you been ignoring areas of sin or compromise in your life?

5. Have you faced struggles and strongholds and worked to gain the victory?

6. Is there anyone with whom you have delayed sharing the truth of the Gospel?

7. If the rapture happened tonight, are you ready? Are those around you ready?

8. After reading this chapter, what is one thing you will put into practice or one thing you will change in your life?

9. How can we, as a group, help you do this?

Chapter 4:

-Punch the mat, get mad at your current state, and find the resolve to fight. _____ _____ _____ the _____!

-Grace, forgiveness, and victory await you from your Heavenly Father. He does not _____ you; He _____.

Write down why you struggle with seeing God as a loving, forgiving father.

_____

_____

_____

_____

_____

_____

_____

Write down five times in your life that God has forgiven you:

1.

2.

3.

4.

5.

Group Study Questions:

1. Are you now or have you ever struggled with getting back up after a spiritual defeat?

2. Do you struggle with seeing God as a loving Father? Why?

3. What will it take for you to finally get angry at being down on the mat?

4. What steps can you take to get back up?

5. Do you want to get back up? Or are you content to stay down and defeated?

6. After reading this chapter, what is one thing you will put into practice or one thing you will change in your life?

7. How can we, as a group, help you do this?

Chapter 5

-There is a constant and ongoing battle between the forces of
_____ and _____ in the spirit world—
_____ _____ and _____
_____.

-As men of God, our passionate pursuit is to walk in _____
total _____.

What part of this chapter convicted you most? Write it down.

_____

_____

_____

_____

_____

_____

_____

_____

Write down three actions you will take to change this area:

1.

2.

3.

Group Study Questions:

1. Do you believe in spiritual warfare? Why or why not?

2. In this chapter, we stated, *"The only two choices that you have are: 'Are you on God's side or Satan's side?' and 'Are you going to 'put on' the weapons God has given you to fight and gain victory, or are you going to run around the spiritual battlefield naked and unprotected?'"* Which choice will you make?

3. In this chapter, we stated, *"As men of God, our passionate pursuit is to walk in God's total victory."* What does this mean, and how can you do it?

4. Will you choose to take your spiritual clothes out of the closet and put them on? Will you rise and get dressed so you can then shine bright to the world?

5. After reading this chapter, what is one thing you will put into practice or one thing you will change in your life?

6. How can we, as a group, help you do this?

Chapter 6

-Truth is_____ — it never _____.

When the enemy attacks us with _____ or _____,
we have faith that God _____ _____ what He said He
_____ _____.

What part of God's clothing have you struggled the most to wear?

_____
_____
_____
_____
_____
_____
_____
_____

Write down four actions you will take to strengthen yourself in this
area.

1.

2.

3.

4.

Group Study Questions:

1. Why is it so important to have spiritual absolutes and truths—things we believe to be true no matter what?

2. What is one area you need to change in your life to walk in holiness and righteousness?

3. What is robbing you of peace in your life? What changes can you make to change this area and gain peace?

4. How does faith protect us from the enemy's attack?

5. How does our salvation guard our minds?

6. Why is the Word of God the primary weapon we have to fight back against attack? Why is it so crucial for us to know God's Word?

7. After reading this chapter, what is one thing you will put into practice or one thing you will change in your life?

8. How can we, as a group, help you do this?

Chapter 7

-Am I a man who is guided by his _____, or do I
_____ and _____ my
_____ when the going gets tough?

-We must identify what _____ _____ and
how far we are willing to go to _____ by those
_____.

-Every time we stand firm in our _____, we grow
_____. Our_____
_____.

Make a list of 6 convictions that you believe that you will not allow
anyone to change your mind about:

1.

2.

3.

4.

5.

6.

Group Study Questions:

1. Why is it so important for a man of God to have personal convictions that we refuse to back down from?

2. Are you a man who is guided by his convictions, or do you flounder and abandon your convictions when the going gets tough?

3. In this chapter, we stated, *"Sit down and make a list of beliefs that you will not compromise on."* What are some of your convictions that you will not back down from?

4. In this chapter, we stated, *"Every time we stand firm in our convictions, we grow stronger. Our convictions deepen."* Have you found this to be true in your life? How?

5. After reading this chapter, what is one thing you will put into practice or one thing you will change in your life?

6. How can we, as a group, help you do this?

Chapter 8

-Our entire purpose in life is to be a _____ light in a _____ world.

-We are the _____ for the person driving down a dark country road. We shine bright for them. We have_____ _____ of the darkness, and we shine the light the _____ needs.

-Our light shows the lost they can have _____. They can experience _____.

Write down three things that stood out to you the most in this chapter:

1.

2.

3.

Group Study Questions:

1. Why is it so important for men of God to show the unsaved trapped in darkness what it is like to live in the light?

2. In this chapter, we spoke about how Egypt was covered in darkness, and only Israel had light. What did you learn from this Bible story?

3. In this chapter, we stated, *"Our light shows them they can have hope. They can experience peace. They can have joy. We show them what they are missing, and we cause them to want what we have."* What does this mean to you?

4. Will you commit yourself to be the light that God has called you to be?

5. Will you shine bright, even when it isn't popular, or goes against cultural norms?

6. Will you do whatever it takes to be God's flashlight in a dark world used to live in utter darkness?

7. After reading this chapter, what is one thing you will put into practice or one thing you will change in your life?

8. How can we, as a group, help you do this?

Chapter 9

-Evolution devalues _____, they devalue the truth that
God created man with a _____ _____.

-The world is full of voices defending this cause or that group. They
are standing up for people of every _____.
_____, and _____…except for
_____.

-One huge way to shine for _____ and stand against
human trafficking is to fight against _____.

What area about shining for light stood out to you the most?

_____

_____

_____

_____

_____

What are some actions you can take to shine bright for this area? List
four:

1.

2.

3.

4.

Group Study Questions:

1. How does evolution devalue life? How does Creationism value life?

2. Why is it so important for a man of God to be opposed to abortion?

3. Why is abortion not a women's health issue, but a life issue?

4. How does sex-trafficking devalue life?

5. What are some actions we, as a group, can take to fight against sex-trafficking?

6. How does pornography devalue life?

7. After reading this chapter, what is one thing you will put into practice or one thing you will change in your life?

8. How can we, as a group, help you do this?

Chapter 10:

-The Bible is _____'s _____ and is still _____ today.

-Sex is for a _____ and _____ only.

-There is a spiritual, dark world. It is run by _____, and he is using it to trap too many believers into

_____.

-We need to help the _____ and _____ find freedom and victory. It is not _____ - _____; it is active and present in today's day and age.

What area about shining for truth stood out to you the most?

_____

_____

_____

What are some actions you can take to shine bright for this area? List four:

1.

2.

3.

4.

Group Study Questions:

1. *In this chapter, we stated, "The words in the Bible are under attack. People don't believe the Bible is relevant today. They feel it is old-fashioned and has no place in today's open, acceptable society."* How have you seen this demonstrated in your sphere of influence?

2. How do we lovingly stand for the Biblical truth that sex is only between a husband and wife?

3. How is Progressive Christianity perverting the truth about sex? How do we combat this?

4. Why is it important to stand for the truth that there is only one true God?

5. What practical changes do you need to make to protect your family from the dangers of the evil, occultic world that is so popular in our society?

6. Are you strong enough to shine bright against today's culture?

7. After reading this chapter, what is one thing you will put into practice or one thing you will change in your life?

8. How can we, as a group, help you do this?

Chapter 11:

-We have _____ a lost and dying world needs, yet we are keeping it to _____ instead of shining bright and giving it to a _____ and _____ world.

-We are the vessel God uses, but _____ is the One Who

_____.

-We _____ keep using a dimmer switch when it comes to healing. Too many people need _____'s _____

_____.

We asked the question, what keeps you from praying for someone's physical healing? What's the worst that could happen? Write down your biggest, worse-case scenario fear.

_____

_____

_____

_____

_____

_____

_____

_____

_____

_____

Now, analyze this list. Answer these questions:

Is the fear realistic?

_____

Is chance of embarrassment worth not taking the chance to see them healed?

_____

Is it your responsibility to heal them, or to pray for them?

_____

Could this simple act of praying for them make them feel cared for even if they aren't healed?

_____

What if God does heal them?

_____

Group Study Questions:

1. Why is it so vital for us to shine bright for healing?

2. What keeps you from asking someone to pray for them when they share a physical issue? What's the worst that could happen?

3. Have you ever experienced a physical healing? Share the story with the group.

4. In this chapter, we stated, _"God heals emotions."_ Why is this turn important? Have you experienced this healing?

5. Why is it so important to allow God to heal our minds?

6. Do you have a relationship that needs to be healed? What can you do to start the healing process?

7. After reading this chapter, what is one thing you will put into practice or one thing you will change in your life?

8. How can we, as a group, help you do this?

Conclusion:

-We must choose once and for all, will we stay in the
_____ of our spiritual _____, or will we
_____ and _____?

-We need to push aside _____, put aside the need for
_____ from others, and decide the only approval we need
is _____'s approval.

A personal note from Jamie:

I believe in you. I believe that you have what it takes. I believe that you have the strength and power to kick back the covers, rise, to shove complacency, fear, and any other thing keeping you stuck under the covers. I believe you have what it takes to rise and shine, to be the beacon of God's light to a lost and dying world.

-Jamie Holden

Will you accept the challenge of this book and rise and shine?

If so, state so below:

I, _____ declare today to except the challenge to rise and shine the truth and hope of God to a lost and dying world. I will no longer burn daylight, I will Rise and Shine

_____   _____

Signature   Date

Group Study Questions:

1. Are you going to throw off the sheets of comfort and complacency and get out of bed?

2. Are you going to stay standing and not allow mistakes or sins you may commit to drive you back to the comfort of the covers?

3. Are you going to daily wear the wardrobe of a man of God that we discussed in chapters five and six?

4. Will you choose to shine bright for God and His ways?

5. Will you develop your own convictions based on God's Word and shine brightly for these convictions?

6. Will you shine for life and embrace the fight in all its forms?

7. Will you shine for truth even when the world tries to convince you that their lies are truth and the Bible's truths are lies?

8. Will you shine for God's healing power to heal bodies, minds, souls, and spirits?

9. Do you have what it takes to rise and shine?

10. After reading this chapter, what is one thing you will put into practice or one thing you will change in your life?

11. How can we, as a group, help you do this?

FILL IN ANSWERS

Chapter One:

- dimming, light

Chapter Two:

- seriously, action
- good enough, faith, Christ
- Great commission

Chapter Three:

- snooze alarm
- rapture, compromising, procrastinating

Chapter Four:

- Get up off, mat
- condemn, forgives

Chapter Five:

- good, evil, God's Kingdom, satan's kingdom
- God's, victory

Chapter Six:

- consistent, changes
- lies, doubts, will do, said, do

Chapter Seven:

- convictions, flounder, abandon, convictions
- believe, stand, beliefs

- convictions, stronger, convictions deepen

Chapter Eight:

- bright, dark
- headlights, come out, darkness, world
- hope, peace

Chapter Nine:

- race, sex, creed, babies
- life, pornography

Chapter Ten:

- God's Word, relevant
- husband, wife
- Satan, darkness
- possessed, oppressed, old-fashioned

Chapter Eleven:

- everything, ourselves, lost hurting
- HE, heals
- CANNOT, God's physical touch

Conclusion:

- comfort, beds, rise, shine
- complacency, approval, God's

Bibliography

Chapter 2

1. Elliott, Belinda. "Saving a Serial Killer", CBN. 30, September, 2020, https://www1.cbn.com/books/saving-a-serial-killer.

Chapter 3

1. Online Alarm Clock. "The History of Snooze Clocks & Why They Are Evil", ONLINECLOCK.net, 30, September, 2020, https://blog.onlineclock.net/evil-snooze-clock-history.

2. Assemblies of God Fundamental Truths. Website: https://ag.org/Beliefs/Statement-of-Fundamental-Truths#13

3. Assemblies of God Positions Paper "The Rapture of the Church" (ADOPTED BY THE GENERAL PRESBYTERY IN SESSION AUGUST 14, 1979)", website: https://ag.org/Beliefs/Position-Papers/The-Rapture-of-the-Church.

Chapter 4

1. *Creed II*. Directed by Steven Caple, performances by Michael B. Jordan, Sylvester Stallone, Tessa Thompson, MGM, Warner Brothers and New Line Cinema. 2018.

Chapter 5

1. Andersen, H C, and Virginia L. Burton. The Emperor's New Clothes. Boston: Houghton Mifflin Co, 1949.

Chapter 6

1.   Evans, Tony. *"The Shoes of Peace"*, Victory in Spiritual Warfare, Eugene, OR, Harvest House Publishers, 2011. Pg 78-80.

2.   *Robin Hood Men in Tights.* Directed by Mel Brooks, performances by Cary Elwes, Richard Lewis, Roger Rees, Amy Yasbeck, Dave Chappelle, Brooksfilms. 1993. Film.

Chapter 7

1. *Captain America: Civil War. Directed by* Russo, Anthony, Joe Russo,   writer: Christopher Markus, Stephen McFeely, Kevin Feige, performances by: Chris Evans, Robert Downey, Scarlett Johansson, Sebastian Stan, Anthony Mackie, Don Cheadle, Jeremy Renner, Chadwick Boseman, Paul Bettany, Elizabeth Olsen, Paul Rudd, Emily VanCamp, Marisa Tomei, Tom Holland, Marvel Studios, 2016. Film.

Chapter 8

1. *"The Dark Knight Rises".* Directed by: Christopher Nolan, performances by Christian Bale, Tom Hardy, Ann Hathaway, Gary Oldman, Joseph Gordon Levitt, Morgan Freeman, Michael Cane.   Warner Brothers Legendary Entertainment, DC Entertainment, 2012. Film.

Chapter 9

1.Assemblies of God Positions Paper "The Doctrine of Creation" (ADOPTED BY THE GENERAL PRESBYTERY IN SESSION AUGUST 20, 2010)", website: https://ag.org/Beliefs/Position-Papers/The-Doctrine-of-Creation

2. Assemblies of God Positions Paper "Sanctity of Human Life: Abortion and Reproductive Issues" (ADOPTED BY THE GENERAL PRESBYTERY IN SESSION AUGUST 9-11, 2010)", website: https://ag.org/Beliefs/Position-Papers/Abortion-Sanctity-of-Human-Life

3. "Putting a Stop to Human Trafficking". Samaritans purse.org, 20, July, 2 0 2 0 , w e b s i t e : h t t p s : / / www.samaritanspurse.org/disaster/putting-a-stop-to-human-trafficking/.

4. Potter, Karen."Open Your Eyes: Porn Is Directly Correlated to Sexual Exploitation". Covenant Eyes. 19, June, 2020, website: https://www.covenanteyes.com/2020/06/19/open-your-eyes-porn-is-directly-correlated-to-sexual-exploitation/.

Chapter 10

1. Castaway. Dir. Robert Zemeckis. Perf. Tom Hanks, Helen Hunt and Nick Searcy. 20th Century Fox and DreamWorks Pictures, 2000. Film.

2. Assemblies of God Core Doctrine "Divine Healing" website: https://ag.org/Beliefs/Our-Core-Doctrines/Divine-Healing.

ALSO AVAILABLE FROM MANTOUR MINISTRIES

**Available in print and digital formats.
Visit www.mantourministries.com
for more information.**

I'd love to come share a challenging word of victory!

DEFEAT IS NOT AN OPTION!

CONTACT ME TO COME SHARE.

Jamie loves to speak to men and is available to speak at your next men's event. Jamie combines humor and his personal testimony to both engage and challenge men to grow in their walk with God. He uses his testimony of overcoming abuse as well as dealing with his physical and emotional issues growing up to encourage men that no matter what their background or where they have come from in life, they can grow into mighty men in God's kingdom.

"Years ago, while I was attending the University of Valley Forge, God gave me a deep desire to minister to men. My calling is to help men learn what it means to be a godly man and how to develop a deep, personal relationship with their heavenly Father. We strive to challenge and encourage men to reach their full potential in God's kingdom."

If you are interested in having Jamie at your next men's event as a speaker or workshop leader, or if you are interested in having him come share with your church, e-mail him at jamie@mantourministries.com. He is also available to speak for one or multiple weeks on the theme of his books, Burning Daylight, Whatever It Takes, Invincible: Scaling The Mountains That Keep Us From Victory. Putting On Manhood, Legacy: Living a Life that Lasts, and Get in the Game.

Will You Partner With Me To Reach Men With The Gospel?

Pray

Please pray for me as I work to reach men inside and outside of the church with the life-changing truth of the Gospel.

Give

Will you consider partnering with me on a monthly basis? Give online at www.giving.ag.org and enter my account number 2813962

Go

Plan to attend your local Mantour Conference.

Jamie Holden
US Missionary Assoc.   Account Number 2813962

GOD IS DOING A MIGHTY WORK IN MEN, YOUR SUPPORT HELPS US FULFILL HIS CALL!

U.S. Missions Faith Promise

Assemblies of God U.S. Missions • 1445 N. Boonville Ave. • Springfield, MO 65802-1894
Phone: (417) 862-2781, ext. 3264 • Fax: (417) 873-9734 • email: AGUSMFinance@ag.org

DONOR INFORMATION

Church   Individual

Name

Address

City   State   Zip

Email   Phone

Account number   Church to credit

Check here if you do not wish to receive promotional materials from U.S. Missions.

RECIPIENT INFORMATION

As the Lord enables us, we promise to invest $_____ each month for support of:

Name of account: **James J. Holden**

Account #: **2813962**   Department: **MAPS**

IMPORTANT: Sign, date, and mail this form today along with your first check, or manage your giving online at www.giving.ag.org. To your faith promise is an agreement between you and God. It is understood that you may revise your promise at any time. God bless you!

U.S. MISSIONS

You Can Give Online At: www.giving.ag.org

FORWARD TO AGUSM

Made in the USA
Middletown, DE
05 April 2021